GUIDE   SELF-STUDY

Torin M. Finser, PhD

GUIDED
SELF-STUDY

**Rudolf Steiner's
Path of
Spiritual
Development**

a workbook for spiritual-scientific study
with excerpts from the works of Rudolf Steiner

SteinerBooks | 2015

2015

STEINERBOOKS

An imprint of Anthroposophic Press, Inc.

610 Main Street, Great Barrington, MA 01230

www.steinerbooks.org

Book design: William Jens Jensen

LIBRARY OF CONGRESS CONTROL NUMBER: 2015934894

ISBN: 978-1-62148-130-0 (paperback)
ISBN: 978-1-62148-131-7 (eBook)

TABLE OF CONTENTS

Introduction

After years of working with the so-called basic (*foundational*) books written by Rudolf Steiner, it has been a great pleasure to go back and reread them all again in light of many years of teaching and life experience. It is amazing how some passages that I've worked with so many times now light up in entirely new ways, given what the reader brings to the activity of study and reflection.

When people refer to the "basic" books, they usually mean texts that Rudolf Steiner himself wrote relatively early on in contrast to transcripts of the many lectures he gave during his life of teaching. The books most often mentioned in this regard are:

- *Intuitive Thinking as a Spiritual Path:*
  A Philosophy of Freedom
- *Theosophy: An Introduction to the Spiritual Processes in Human Life and in the Cosmos*
- *How to Know Higher Worlds:*
  A Modern Path of Initiation
- *An Outline of Esoteric Science*

The last of these contains chapters reworked from portions of *Theosophy* and *How to Know Higher Worlds,* with the significant addition of chapter four describing evolution. Rudolf Steiner waited some years before writing that fourth chapter, and for a variety of reasons I have decided not to include it in this guided self-study (at Antioch University New England, for instance, we have an entire course on that chapter). Instead, a couple of chapters from my book *Organizational Integrity* have been included here that could be considered a mild introduction to the theme of evolution. Thus, the material for this guided study mainly involves the first three books plus a few supplements intended to help the learning process.

For whom is this book intended? I have imagined two potential audiences:

1. There are those who are interested in becoming Waldorf school teachers, Camphill coworkers, or biodynamic farmers, who want and need an introduction to the philosophy behind these and other initiatives arising from Anthroposophy. In addition, Waldorf schools and Camphill communities often hire administrative personnel who have expertise in one particular area or another but do not have a background in Anthroposophy. They may not have the time or ability to travel to a place where an anthroposophic foundation studies program is offered, yet they want some guidance rather than simply "reading the books." This guided self-study is intended to be "user friendly," in that one can take up small sections of the text at a time, reflect, and then answer a question before moving on. This book, especially in eBook format, may be the only way some people can work with the material if they live in geographical areas far removed from Waldorf schools or other anthroposophic communities.

2. Similarly, for the second group of intended users, there are those who hear about the work of Rudolf Steiner, Anthroposophy, or one of the anthroposophic initiatives and want to learn more, especially before considering membership in the Anthroposophical Society. A text such as this might be helpful as one of many possible options (such as attending conferences, workshops, visiting, etc.) that are available to those at the "beginner" stage. Incidentally, I use the quotes around *"beginner"* intentionally, as I have found that questions from a beginner's mind are often the most profound, and there can be much wisdom residing in a human being just waiting to be released.

First, one might ask: Why not just read the first three books? After all, Rudolf Steiner wrote them in such a way that the very act of reading them can awaken new faculties. Who could ever duplicate that? It might even seem presumptuous to select passages from books that were constructed by an initiate. To those who have these and other objections, I have the following response: My hope is that the pages in this book serve as an *invitation, so that those who work with this material will then be motivated to go to the original texts and work with them more intensively.*

We all have particular tasks in life. One of mine is bridge building. That is why I work in a university setting, why I travel extensively, and why my books are all directed toward those who are trying to find a connection to Waldorf education, Anthroposophy, or related work. I feel that those of us who have access to spiritual treasures have an obligation to make them available to humankind. Rudolf Steiner was explicit in this regard. He was deeply interested in all the contemporary trends around him and enjoyed meeting and working with people who were new to his worldview. Anthroposophy is a modern path of transformation, and it can be an open book for those who take an interest.

So I hope what follows can be seen as an invitation and an open book that encourages self-development and contemplation. To this end, I have selected passages that contain key points, followed by a question or two. There are no "correct answers" to the questions as there are in an SAT test, for example. More important is inner engagement and an ability to relate the content to one's own soul life. Have I experienced something like this? How does this sit with me? Am I able to relate what I find to my own life or that of my friends? One might say I am trying to promote inner dialogue, for the best form of education is indeed self-education.

If a person is interested in applying to a teacher-training program or wishes to connect with a Waldorf school, Camphill, etc., working with these passages can form a backdrop to an interview conversation. In some cases, one might be asked to read additional books, or complete workshops, but work with this guided self-study can be seen as the first step.

There are two aspects of preparation that cannot be fulfilled through this self-study:

1. There is great value in group conversation and the social/pedagogical dynamic of learning with others. One can perhaps exchange emails or get together with a friend to share some of the experiences while following this guided study, but there is no substitute for actual group experience. Thus, if this book becomes the basis of one's first steps, I strongly advise that the next steps, such as actual teacher training, be done in a face-to-face program and not online. Our world today needs socially adept people more than ever, and some things can be practiced only through group work.

2. Working with the passages in this self-study does not involve any of the arts that are essential to personal and professional transformation. In an anthroposophic context, these may include the arts of eurythmy, music, speech and drama, painting, clay modeling, storytelling, etc. I strongly recommend that those interested in further work seek out workshops offered around the country that focus on some of these arts. They are offered at many Waldorf schools and at the adult-education institutes such as Antioch University New England, Center for Anthroposophy, Rudolf Steiner College, Rudolf Steiner Centre in Toronto, etc. There is also much value in simple participation in local art activities such as a community chorus, learning to play an instrument, participating in a dramatic production, and so on.

When I interview applicants at Antioch, I am more interested in *whether* someone has done artistic work and how far they have gone, versus which ones. There is a reason that Waldorf has been described as *the art of teaching.*

Finally, a few words about the construction of this book. Each section represents the content of another of the foundational books as described. At the end of each section we have included a complete lecture by Rudolf Steiner, in which he *applies* some of the concepts covered in the other readings. For example, the lecture on the four temperaments includes a practical application of the fourfold human being described in *Theosophy.* One could say that the lectures at the end of a section are an application of the theory, as well as a kind of friendly test of how much one has really understood. Finally, I have included several appendices to provide additional material for those who want to try alternatives or sample different perspectives.

We plan to do small print runs and edit the text in response to our readers. So please let me and/or SteinerBooks know how this works for you and how we can improve the experience for those that follow in your footsteps.

On behalf of the community of spirit seekers around the world, welcome to this work!

Torin M. Finser
Keene, New Hampshire
2015

Acknowledgements

I would like to thank my colleagues, especially Hugh Renwick, Arthur Auer, and Karine Munk Finser for their support, especially for reviewing the content of specific sections of this book.

I am deeply grateful to my Antioch research assistant, Rebecca Brown, for her dedicated work in typing, copying and pasting, reviewing and editing questions, and many other tasks too varied to list here. She has accompanied this project for many months, always cheerfully and with goodwill.

I would also like to thank SteinerBooks and their donors for supporting this work. As I have often stated, we need freedom of speech and freedom of choice, both of which are possible only with a free press and independent publishers.

PART I

EXCERPTS FROM THE WORKS OF RUDOLF STEINER WITH GUIDING QUESTIONS

CHAPTER 1

THE BOOK OF PEACE

Excerpts from *How to Know Higher Worlds*
by Rudolf Steiner

1. HOW TO KNOW HIGHER WORLDS

The capacities by which we can gain insights into higher worlds lie dormant within each one of us.

From the beginning of the human race, a form of schooling has always existed in which persons possessing higher faculties guide those who seek to develop these faculties for themselves. Such schooling is called esoteric or mystery schooling; and the instruction one receives there is called esoteric, or occult, teaching.

In actuality, esoteric or inner knowledge is no different from other kinds of human knowledge and ability. It is a mystery for the average person only to the extent that writing is a mystery for those who have not yet learned to write. Just as, given the right teaching methods, anyone can learn to write, so too anyone can become a student of esoteric knowledge, and, yes, even a teacher of it, if he or she follows the appropriate path. Ordinary knowledge and ability differ from esoteric knowledge in one respect only. A person may not have the possibility of learning to write because of the cultural conditions or poverty he or she is born

3

into, but no one who seeks sincerely will find any barriers to achieving knowledge and abilities in the higher worlds.

There is a universal law among initiates that the knowledge due a seeker cannot be withheld. Nevertheless, there is another universal law that esoteric knowledge may not be imparted to anyone not qualified to receive it. ❧ → *Receptive*

In ancient, prehistoric times, the temples of the spirit were outwardly visible, but today, when our life has become so unspiritual, they no longer exist where we can see them with our physical eyes. Yet spiritually they are still present everywhere, and whoever seeks can find them. We begin with a fundamental mood of soul. Spiritual researchers call this basic attitude the path of reverence, of devotion to truth and knowledge.

If you have ever stood before the door of someone you revered, filled with holy awe as you turned the doorknob to enter for the first time a room that was a "holy place" for you, then the feeling you experienced at that moment is the seed that can later blossom into your becoming a student in an occult, esoteric school. To be gifted with the potential for such feelings is a blessing for every young person.

A child's reverence for others develops into a reverence for truth and knowledge. Experience teaches that we know best how to hold our heads high in freedom if we have learned to feel reverence when it is appropriate—and it is appropriate whenever it flows from the depths of the heart.

Only a person who has passed through the gate of humility can ascend to the heights of the spirit.

Our civilization is more inclined to criticize, judge, and condemn than to feel devotion and selfless veneration. Our children *thought to* criticize far more than they respect or revere. But just as surely as every feeling of devotion and reverence nurtures the soul's

↳ *because they are often criticized...*

4

powers for higher knowledge, so every act of criticism ~~and judg-ment~~ drives these powers away. ···.??? *it's about looking inward, not outward. First for TRUTH*

The price of this gain in outer culture has been a corresponding loss in higher knowledge and spiritual life. Therefore, we must never forget that higher knowledge has to do with revering truth and insight and not with revering people. *why not celebrating the divine in human? always good...*

In times when the material conditions of life were still simple, spiritual progress was easier. What was revered and held sacred *was it???* stood out more clearly from the rest of the world. In an age of *But maybe have been wrong...* criticism, on the other hand, ideals are degraded. Reverence, awe, adoration, and wonder are replaced by other feelings—they are pushed more and more into the background. As a result, everyday life offers very few opportunities for their development. Anyone seeking higher knowledge must create these feelings inwardly, instilling them in the soul. This cannot be done by studying. (It can be done only by living.) *→ TRUE .*

Experienced spiritual researchers know what strength they gain by always looking for the good in everything and withholding their critical judgment. This practice should not remain simply an outer rule of life, but must take hold of the innermost part of the soul. It lies in our hands to perfect ourselves and gradually transform ourselves completely. But this transformation must take place in our innermost depths, in our thinking. *TRUE.* Showing respect outwardly in our relations with other beings is not ~~enough~~ *nothing*; we must carry this respect into our thoughts. Therefore, we must begin our inner schooling by bringing devotion into our thought life. We must *release* ~~guard~~ against disrespectful, disparaging, and criticizing thoughts. We must ~~try to~~ practice reverence ~~and devotion~~ in our thinking at all times. *→ allow the guidance to come from within or where to devote.*

(Just as the Sun's rays quicken all living things, so the reverence in us quickens all the feelings in our soul. *???*

I think ⊕ in mind allows us to hear the upwelling echos of ♡ from our innermost being and the world around us.

[handwritten margin notes at top: "think the soul is always very bright + perfect, no matter what we do. We're mired in 'criticism,' we're disconnected from it."]

We nourish it with reverence, respect, and devotion. These make the soul healthy and strong, particularly for the activity of knowing. Disrespect, antipathy, and disparaging admirable things, on the other hand, paralyze and ~~slay~~ our cognitive activities. *[handwritten: shift] [handwritten: to tumble places]*

> 1. *Share an example or two of instances in which you experienced reverence, respect, or devotion. This might have occurred while on a walk in nature, while attending a concert, reading a poem, or seeing a beautiful painting. Give an example or two and then share how you felt in that moment. Likewise, if you have ever been criticized, how did you feel at that time?*

[handwritten left margin note: "Point converts to the stillness of answers. Surround, surround with & light. and find the divine answers."]

What we attain through devotion becomes even more effective when another kind of feeling is added. This consists in our learning to surrender ourselves less and less to the impressions of the outer world and develop instead an active inner life. If we chase after amusements and rush from one sense impression to the next, we will not find the way to esoteric knowledge. As students of esoteric knowledge, we are told to create moments in life when we can withdraw into ourselves in silence and solitude. In these moments, we should not give ourselves up to our own concerns. To do so would lead to the opposite of what we are striving for. Instead, in such moments, we should allow what we have experienced—what the outer world has told us—to linger on in utter stillness. In these quiet moments, every flower, every animal, and every action will disclose mysteries undreamed of. This prepares us to receive new sense impressions of the outer world with eyes quite different than before.

Every insight that you seek only to enrich your own store of learning and to accumulate treasure for yourself alone leads

---

*   Questions have been inserted into the text by Torin Finser to stimulate the reader's attention to various points in Rudolf Steiner's text.

6

you from your path, but every insight that you seek in order to become more mature on the path of the ennoblement of human- ity and world evolution brings you one step forward. *which require confronting your concerns.*

Every idea that does not become an ideal for you kills a force in your soul, but every idea that becomes an ideal for you ~~creates~~ *shapes & directs* forces of life within you. *??? Split focus? I disagree. or = doesn't kill you.*

2. Consider this for a while and share how this might be related to your development as a human being. *part of your journey.*

Regulate each of your words and actions so that you do not interfere with anyone's free decisions and will.

Create moments of inner peace for yourself, and in these moments learn to distinguish the essential from the inessential.

As students of the spirit, we must set aside a brief period of time in daily life in which to focus on things that are quite differ- ent from the objects of our daily activity. The kind of activity we engage in must also differ from what occupies the rest of our day. *need help for disagreement... ?*

In these moments we should tear ourselves completely out of our everyday life. Our thinking and feeling lives should have a quite different coloring than they usually have. We should allow our joys, sorrows, worries, experiences, and actions to pass before our soul. But our attitude toward these should be one of looking at everything we have experienced from a higher point of view. *yes.*

In the time we have set aside for ourselves, then, we must strive to view and judge our own experiences and actions as though they belonged to another person. *→ Removing yourself again. why? Distancing yourself*

As students of higher knowledge we must find the strength to view ourselves as we would view strangers. We must face our- selves with the inner tranquility of a judge. If we achieve this, our own experiences will reveal themselves in a new light. As long as we are still woven into our experiences, and stand within them, we will remain as attached to the nonessential as to the essential.

if you can't allow for change ... how do you allow for change from you; intuition?

→ true. But ... I have to silence my inner judge. I don't have to worry about that of strangers.

But once we have attained the inner peace of the overview, the nonessential separates itself from the essential. Sorrow and joy, every thought, every decision will look different when we stand over against ourselves in this way.

The value of such inner, peace-filled self-contemplation depends less upon what one contemplates and more upon finding the inner strength that such inner calm develops. For all human beings, in addition to what we may call the ordinary, everyday self, also bear within themselves a higher self or higher human being. This higher human being remains concealed until it is awakened. *weird split - can cause a dis owning or disavowing of higyurself...??*

3. Set aside time each day to practice the suggestions from the foregoing paragraphs, distinguishing the essential from the inessential, looking at oneself as one would a stranger, and developing inner calm and perspective. After working in this way on cultivating an inner life, share a few sentences as to your successes and struggles.

Our whole being becomes more peaceful. We act with greater confidence and certainty in all our undertakings. We do not lose composure in the face of all kinds of events. Slowly, as we continue on the path, we increasingly come to guide ourselves, as it were, rather than allowing ourselves to be led by circumstances and outer influences. Before long, we realize that the moments set aside each day are a great source of strength for us. For example, we gradually cease to become angry about the things that used to annoy us, and are no longer afraid of many things that used to frighten us.

As we progress in this direction, we become increasingly able to control the effect that impressions from the outer world have upon us. For example, we may hear someone say something to hurt or anger us. Before we began esoteric training, this would have made us feel hurt or anger. Now, however, because we are on the path of inner development, we can take the hurtful or annoying sting out of another's words before it finds its way into our inner being.

The impatience that was about to take root thus disappears, and the time we would otherwise have wasted in expressions of impatience can now be filled with some useful observation that we may make while we wait.

> *4. Share an example from your everyday life in which you were prevented from doing something when you had planned to do it. How did it feel? Did you experience impatience? While waiting, were you able to make a useful observation instead of simply feeling impatience?*

Ethiopia -- ! ! ! ! lol.

As long as the outer being has the upper hand and guides us, the "inner" self remains its slave and cannot unfold its powers. If other people can make me angry, I am not the master of myself—*truth,* (or rather, better stated, I have not yet found the "inner ruler." *such.* In other words, I must develop the inner faculty of allowing the impressions of the outer world to reach me only in ways that I myself have chosen. Only if I do this, can I become a student of the esoteric. Only a person striving sincerely for this ability can reach the goal. How far we advance in a certain amount of time is unimportant; what matters is only that our seeking be sincere. Many work on themselves for years without noticeable progress, and then suddenly—if they have not despaired, but have remained unshakable—they attain the "inner victory." *—keeps point-ed...*

(On the path to knowledge all depends upon whether we can face ourselves and all our deeds and actions energetically, with inner truthfulness and uncompromising honesty, as though we were strangers to ourselves. *)true.*

Removed from our daily round, we become deaf to its noise. Everything around us grows still. We put aside everything that reminds us of outer impressions. Quiet, inward contemplation and dialog with the purely spiritual world completely fill our soul. For students of the spirit, this quiet contemplation must become a necessity of life. At first, we are wholly absorbed in a world of thought. We must develop a living feeling for this silent thinking activity. We must learn to love what streams toward us from the spirit.

We experience that life speaks in this world of thoughts. We realize that thoughts are not mere shadow pictures and that hidden beings speak to us through thoughts. Out of the silence something begins to speak to us. Previously we could hear speech only with our ears, but now words resound in our souls. An inner speech, an inner word, is disclosed to us. The first time we experience this we feel supremely blessed.

This path teaches us that the most trivial tasks we have to carry out and the most trivial experiences that come our way are woven together with great cosmic beings and world events. *more*

When we raise ourselves through meditation to what unites us with the spirit, we quicken *connect w/* something within us that is eternal and unlimited by birth and death. Once we have experienced this eternal part in us, we can no longer doubt its existence. Meditation is thus the way to knowing and beholding the eternal, indestructible, essential center of our being. Only meditation can lead us to this vision.

> *5. Have you had experience with meditation prior to meeting Anthroposophy and the texts in this book? If so, what were they? If not, are you interested in developing your higher self through cultivating an inner life?*

2. THE STAGES OF INITIATION

The first step is to direct the soul's attention toward certain processes in the world around us. These processes are life, as it buds, grows, and flourishes; and, on the other hand, all phenomena connected with withering, fading, and dying away.

First, we must look at things as actively and precisely as possible. Only thereafter should we devote ourselves to the feelings coming to life in our souls and the thoughts arising there. It is essential that we give our attention to both feelings and thoughts as they arise in complete inner equilibrium.

Whoever repeatedly directs his or her attention to processes of becoming, flourishing, and blossoming will feel something faintly resembling the sensation we experience as we watch the sunrise. Processes of withering and dying, on the other hand, will produce an experience that may be compared with what we feel as we watch the slow rise of the Moon on the horizon.

Let things themselves tell us their meaning.

> 6. Practice this exercise: take a leaf or flower and devote your full attention to uninterrupted observation. Then do the same with an old stick or dead leaf. What do you experience inwardly? What are the differences in your feelings and thoughts when you move from the one object to the other?

Feelings and thoughts are actual facts, just as real as tables and chairs are in the physical-sensory world.

To move forward on the path to higher knowledge and advance in Spiritual Science, we must therefore pay as careful attention to our thoughts and feelings as we do to our movements in the physical world. For instance, we do not usually try to go straight through a wall, but direct our steps around it; that is, we

[handwritten margin note top: restrictive. why fight it? shift focus instead.]

[handwritten margin note left: That seems unnecessarily]

comply with the laws of the physical world. The world of feelings and thoughts likewise has its own laws, but they do not force themselves upon us from the outside. Rather, they must flow out of the life of the soul. For this to occur, we must never allow ourselves false thoughts and feelings. Random musings, playful daydreams, and the arbitrary ebb and flow of feeling—all these must be banished from the soul. We need not fear that this will make us unfeeling. On the contrary, we will find that only when we regulate our inner life in this way do we become truly rich in feelings and creative in genuine imagination. Important feelings and fruitful thoughts will then take the place of petty indulgence in emotions and the playful association of ideas. These, in turn, will help us to orient ourselves in the spiritual world, thereby allowing us to enter into a right relationship with the things in it.

The students of esoteric knowledge must also direct their attention to the world of sounds. Here we must distinguish between sounds produced by so-called inanimate objects (such as a falling object, a bell, or a musical instrument) and those coming from living beings (animals or human beings). If we hear a bell, we perceive the sound and associate it with a pleasant feeling.

The scream of an animal, on the other hand, not only evokes an emotional association but also reveals the animal's inner experience, its pleasure, or its pain. In esoteric training, we focus on the second type of sound, concentrating our whole attention on the fact that the sound communicates something that lies outside our own souls. *[handwritten: But animals communicate nonverbally...]*

[handwritten margin note: ? ?]

We must immerse ourselves in this "otherness," inwardly uniting our feelings with the pain or pleasure expressed by the sound. To do this, we must disregard what the sound is for us—whether it is pleasant or unpleasant, agreeable or disagreeable. Our soul must be filled only with what is happening in the being from whom the sound comes. If we practice this exercise systematically and deliberately, we will acquire as we do so the faculty of merging, as it were, with the being that made the sound.

> 7. Decide to adopt a "day of sound" in which you do all the normal things but listen especially intently to the sounds around you. What do they reveal? What can one learn by listening more attentively?

Particularly important as we develop as esoteric pupils is that we also work on the way we listen to other people when they speak. On the path to higher knowledge this listening skill is extremely important. We must become accustomed to listening in such a way that we quiet our own inner life completely when we listen. For example, when someone expresses an opinion and another listens, agreement or disagreement usually stirs immediately within the listener. Often in such a situation we feel compelled to express our own opinion at once, especially if we disagree. However, on the path to higher knowledge we must learn to silence any agreement or disagreement with the opinions we hear.

Not only must we silence our intellectual judgment but also any feelings of disapproval, rejection, or even agreement. Above all, we must observe ourselves carefully to ensure that such feelings, even though absent from the surface of the soul, are not present in its innermost depths. For example, we must learn to listen to the remarks of those who are in some way inferior to us, suppressing every feeling of superiority or knowing better. Listening to children in this way is especially useful, and even the wisest of us can learn a great deal from them.

> 8. Why is it so hard to become inwardly silent?

We begin to learn how to unite ourselves with the being of the other person and fully enter into it. We begin to hear through the words, into the other person's soul. As we consistently practice this new habit, sound becomes the medium through which we can perceive soul and spirit. This practice requires the strictest self-discipline, but it also leads to a lofty goal.

Reading such writings and listening to the teachings of esoteric researchers are themselves a means of achieving knowledge for ourselves. Indeed, every statement of Spiritual Science that we hear is intended to guide the mind in the direction it must take if the soul is to experience any true progress. Therefore the exercises described here should be accompanied by the intensive study of what researchers in spiritual science bring into the world. Such study is part of the preparatory work in all schools of esoteric training.

These teachings are drawn forth from the living "inner word," from "living inspiration," and therefore they themselves are spiritually alive. They are not just words. They are living forces. And as we follow the words of one experienced in esoteric knowledge or read a book based on true inner experience, forces are at work in our souls that make us seers (clairvoyants), just as the forces of nature have shaped our eyes and ears out of living matter.

First, we try to direct our whole attention to comparing a stone and an animal. The thoughts that we form to make this comparison must pass through the soul accompanied by lively feelings. No other thoughts or feelings must be allowed to intrude and disturb our intense, attention-filled observation. We should say to ourselves: "The stone has a form. The animal also has a form. The stone stays peacefully in its place. The animal changes its place."

As we immerse ourselves intensely in these thoughts, observing stone and animal with close attention, two very different kinds of feeling come to life in the soul. One kind streams into the soul from the stone, another from the animal.

If we add plants to our observations, we notice that the feeling streaming from a plant, both in its nature and intensity, lies midway between what streams from a stone and what streams from an animal. The organs built up in this way are spiritual eyes. They gradually allow us to see soul and spiritual colors. But as long as we have not made our own what was previously described as the path or stage of "preparation," the lines and figures of the spiritual world remain dark. Through the process of illumination, they become light.

> 9. When you quietly observe a stone, and then a plant and an animal, do you experience different feelings? If so, how could you describe them? If not, try again.

One precaution, at all events, is essential, and whoever is unwilling to adopt it had better not proceed in esoteric science at all. As esoteric students, we must not lose any of our human qualities but must remain noble-minded, good people, sensitive to all aspects of physical reality. In fact, throughout the course of our esoteric training, we must continuously increase our moral strength, inner integrity, and faculty of observation. During the basic exercises, for example, we must seek to enlarge not only our compassion for the human and animal worlds but also our sense for the beauty of nature. If we do not bear this in mind, then both these feelings and our aesthetic sense will be dulled by the exercises. Our heart will become hard, our senses blunted. Clearly, this would have dangerous consequences.

What happens in the stage of illumination after we have practiced the stone, plant, and animal exercises and have risen to a consideration of the human being, and how, after illumination, the soul unites with the spiritual world under all circumstances and so is led to initiation—all this, the next sections will describe, insofar as it is possible to do so.

Many people abandon the path to esoteric knowledge soon after embarking upon it because they do not notice any immediate progress. Students often mistake their first perceptible higher experiences for illusions when these do not correspond with what they had expected. Such students lose courage because they consider their first experiences worthless or because these experiences seem insignificant and unlikely to lead to anything more valuable in the foreseeable future.

Courage and self-confidence are two beacons that should never be extinguished on the path to higher knowledge. No one, who cannot patiently repeat an exercise that has failed, to all appearances, countless times before, will travel far on this path.

"Within my own feelings and thoughts the highest mysteries lie concealed, but until now I have not perceived them."

The esoteric student must become as conscious of soul and spirit as the ordinary person is of his or her body. It all comes down to giving our feelings and thoughts the right direction. Only then can we gain the ability to see what ordinarily remains invisible. One of the ways of achieving this will be given here.

> 10. Most of the time in daily life we let our thoughts and feelings waft through us in a random way. Self-development at this early stage is all about learning to give direction to our inner life and consciously working with our thoughts and feelings. Here is the next step:

We place before us a small seed from a plant. Starting with this insignificant thing, the point will be to think the right thoughts intensively, and by means of these thoughts to develop certain feelings. First, we must establish what we are really seeing with our eyes. We describe to ourselves the form, color, and other properties of the seed. Then we ponder the thought: "This seed, if planted in the ground, will grow into a complex plant." We visualize the plant, we make it present to and in us. We build it up in imagination. Then we think: "What I now visualize in my imagination, forces of earth and light will later in reality draw forth from this small seed. But if this were an artificial seed, an artificial copy so perfect that my eyes could not distinguish it from a real seed, then no forces of earth and light would ever be able to draw forth such a plant from it." If we can clearly form this thought and bring it to life within us, then we will be able to form the next thought easily and with the right feeling: "Within the seed already lies concealed what—as the force of the whole plant—later grows out of it. The artificial copy of the seed has no such force. Yet, to my eyes, both seeds look the same. Therefore, the real seed contains something invisible that is absent in the copy."

We should hold the thought: "The invisible will become visible. If I were unable to think, then what later becomes visible could not announce itself to me now."

It is important to emphasize that whatever we think we must also feel with intensity. Meditative thoughts need to be experienced calmly and peacefully. No other thoughts should distract us. Time should be allowed for both the thought, and the feeling united with it, to penetrate the soul. If this is done in the right way, then after a time—perhaps only after many unsuccessful attempts—we become conscious of a new force within us. This creates a new perception. The seed seems to be enclosed in a small cloud of light. In a sensory and spiritual way, we sense it as a kind of flame. At its center, we experience a sensation similar to the impression made by the color purple, at its edges a sensation similar to the color blue. What we could not see before now becomes apparent to us, created by the force of the thoughts and feelings that we have awakened within us. The plant—which is still physically invisible and will not become visible until later—is revealed to us in a spiritually visible way.

> 11. How could it help us in a variety of professions (as teachers, nurses, farmers, etc.) if we are able to develop "new perception"? How could this help us better serve humanity?

A further exercise, connected to the seed meditation, is the following. We place before us a mature plant. First, we immerse ourselves in the thought: "A time will come when this plant will wither and decay. Everything I see now will then no longer exist. But the plant will have produced seeds, and these will become new plants. Thus, once again I become aware that something I cannot see lies hidden in what I can see." We saturate ourselves with the thought: "The plant form with all its colors will soon no longer be there. But the knowledge that the plant produces seeds teaches me that it will not disappear into nothingness. I cannot see what preserves the plant from disappearance any more than I could see the future plant in the seed. Therefore, it follows that there is something in the plant, too, that I cannot see with my eyes. But if I let this thought live within me, and the appropriate feeling unites with it, then after a time new force will grow in my soul and become a new perception." A kind of spiritual flame form will then grow out of the plant. Of course, this flame will be correspondingly larger than the one described in the case of the seed. It will be felt as green-blue at its center and as yellow-red at its periphery. Again, it must be strongly emphasized that we do not see what are here called "colors" in the same way that we see colors with our physical eyes. Rather, through spiritual perception we experience something similar to the impression made by physical colors.

For the spirit, birth and death are merely transformations, just as the burgeoning of a bud into a blossom is a transformation occurring before our physical eyes. To come to know this first-hand through our own spiritual vision, we must first awaken spiritual senses for it in the way indicated here.

12. How are birth and death a transformation?

"For every single step that you take in seeking knowledge of hidden truths, you must take three steps in perfecting your character toward the good." We visualize a person whom we have observed longing for something, and we direct our attention to this desire. It is best to recall the moment when the desire was strongest, and we did not yet know whether the person would obtain the object of their desire. Then we surrender ourselves to this picture, completely dedicated to what we can observe in our memory. We create the greatest imaginable inner calm in our souls. We try as far as possible to be deaf and blind to everything else going on around us. Above all, we pay close attention to any feeling that the mental image we have formed awakens in our souls. Then we allow this feeling to rise up within us, like a cloud on an otherwise empty horizon.

> 13. This is the 3:1 rule of spiritual development: we need to strive to take three steps in character development for every one we take in knowledge of spiritual worlds. Knowledge without moral development/self-development can lead to arrogance and even destruction. Why?

Here, then, is another important rule for the student of esoteric knowledge: "Know how to be silent about your spiritual perceptions. Yes, even be silent about them with yourself. Do not try to clothe in words what you see in the spirit, nor try to understand it with your ordinary, unskilled reason. Give yourself fully to your spiritual perception, and do not disturb it with too much pondering. Remember that your thinking is not yet on the level of your spiritual vision.

The above exercise may be supplemented by the following complementary one. This time we contemplate a person whose desire or longing has been fulfilled. Following the same rules and precautions as before, we attain another, different spiritual perception. We again see a spiritual flame-form, but now this feels yellow in the center and light green at the periphery.

Candidates for initiation must bring with them two additional qualities: courage and fearlessness. These have a certain relationship with each other and must be developed together. As esoteric students, we must deliberately seek out situations in which these virtues may be cultivated. Indeed, in esoteric training they are developed quite systematically. From this point of view, life itself is also a good esoteric school—perhaps the best. We must be able to look danger calmly in the eye and overcome difficulties without hesitation. When facing a danger, we should immediately be stirred to the conviction: "All fear is useless. I must not let it take hold of me. I must think only of what is to be done." In fact, we must reach a point, in situations that earlier would have caused us to be afraid, in which the very idea of fear and lack of courage become things impossible for us to conceive in the core of our soul. Such self-education in courage and fearlessness develops quite specific forces that we need for initiation into higher knowledge.

14. Can you give an example or two of how you have learned to overcome a fear, and how courage can arise from such life experience?

The world's powers are both destructive and constructive; the fate of sense-perceptible beings is to arise and pass away. The initiate must see and understand how these forces and this fate work themselves out. For this, the veil that lies before our spiritual eyes in ordinary life must be removed. Of course, we ourselves are closely interwoven with these forces and with fate. Our individual natures, like the world, contain destructive and constructive forces. As initiates, our own souls will be revealed before our seeing eyes as nakedly as all other things. Students must not lose strength in the face of such self-knowledge. They must come to meet it with a surplus of forces. In order to have this surplus, we must learn to maintain our inward calm and certainty in difficult life situations and cultivate an unshakable trust in the good powers of existence. We should be prepared for the fact that many motives that have previously guided us can no longer do so. We shall have to realize that we thought and did many things simply because we were caught up in ignorance. The grounds we had for doing things no longer hold good. We may often have acted out of conceit, but we now come to realize how unspeakably useless all vanity is to the initiate. We have been motivated by greed; now we realize how destructive greed is. We have to develop completely new grounds for acting and thinking.

15. Courage and fearlessness are essential for gaining access to the spiritual worlds and attaining a state of expanded consciousness.

3. INITIATION

If we were initiated today, without preparation, we would lack the experiences we would otherwise continue to gather through future incarnations up to the moment when, as part of the normal course of our development, these mysteries were revealed to us. As we arrive at the doorway to initiation, these experiences must be replaced by something else. Therefore, the first instructions given to candidates for initiation form a substitute for future experiences they would have had in lives to come. These instructions concern the so-called "trials" through which a candidate must pass. The trials themselves arise as the natural consequence of our soul life when the exercises described in the previous chapters have been practiced in the right way.

The first trial consists in achieving a truer perception than the average person possesses of the physical properties, initially of inanimate bodies, and then of plants, animals, and human beings. This has nothing to do with what is called "scientific knowledge." We are not concerned here with science, but with "perception." As a rule, the procedure is one in which, as candidates for initiation, we learn to recognize how natural things and living beings reveal themselves to our spiritual ears and eyes. In a certain sense, these things stand before us unveiled—or naked. The qualities that we come to see and hear were veiled from our physical sight and hearing. The fact that during initiation this veil falls away is due to a process called "the process of spiritual burning away." For this reason, the first trial is called the Fire Trial.

For many people, ordinary life itself is already a more or less unconscious process of initiation through the fire trial. Such people have lived a life so rich in experiences that their self-confidence, courage, and steadfastness have matured in healthy ways; they have learned to bear suffering, disappointment, and failure calmly, magnanimously, and with unbroken strength. People who have worked through their experiences in this way are often already, although without knowing it clearly, initiates. It then takes only a little to open their spiritual eyes and ears so that they become seers. One thing is certain: the purpose of the real fire trial is not to satisfy our curiosity. To be sure, we shall come to know extraordinary facts that other people have no inkling of. But acquaintance with such facts is not the objective; it is but the means to an end. The objective is to acquire truer self-confidence, greater courage, and quite a different kind of magnanimity and endurance than is normally attainable within the lower world.

Rather, it is as if we grow toward clairvoyant knowing, and while we grow, there develops in us—as a soul faculty—a force impelling us to decipher, as if they were the characters of a script, the events and beings of the spiritual world present before us. As our inner development unfolds, it can happen that this power, and the experience of the trial connected with it, appear on their own. However, we shall be more likely to reach our goal if we follow the instructions of experienced esoteric researchers, who are proficient in deciphering the hidden script.

The signs of this esoteric writing are not arbitrarily devised but correspond to the forces at work in the world. Through these signs we learn the language of things. As candidates for initiation we realize immediately that these signs correspond to the figures, colors, and sounds that we learned to perceive in the earlier stages of preparation and illumination. It becomes apparent that all that came before was like learning the letters of the alphabet in order to spell. But now we begin to read in the higher world. All that previously appeared only in isolated figures, sounds, and colors now appears as one great connected and interrelated whole. For the first time we experience complete certainty in our observation of the higher worlds.

There are people who perform such actions unconsciously, without having undergone an esoteric training. These "helpers of the world and humanity" pass through life bestowing blessings and good deeds wherever they go. For reasons that will not be discussed here, they have been endowed with gifts that seem supernatural. They differ from those following the path to higher knowledge only in that the latter act consciously, understanding the larger context of their actions. What we, as esoteric students, achieve through training and esoteric practice, the higher powers bestow on these blessed people for the benefit of the whole world.

The [next] trial is called the Water Trial because when we act in these higher realms, outer circumstances no longer "support" us, just as we lose the ground under our feet when we swim in deep water. This practice should be repeated until we have complete confidence in our abilities.

This trial provides us with abundant opportunities for the development of self-control, which is of prime importance. The trial will thus be easier for those who have acquired self-control in their lives before initiation. Those who can follow high principles and ideals, regardless of personal feelings and desires—who understand the need to perform duties even when inclinations and sympathies turn them in another direction—are already and without knowing it initiates in ordinary life. For such people, passing this second trial will be an easy matter.

Our wishes, desires, and inclinations do not change the realities of the physical world, but they have a real effect on things in the higher worlds. To produce a particular effect in the higher worlds, therefore, we must have complete power over ourselves—we must be able to follow the right discipline and not be subject to our own arbitrariness.

An important human quality that enters into consideration above all else at this stage of initiation is an unconditionally sound, reliable power of judgment.

All preconceptions and cherished beliefs must disappear; truth alone must be the guiding principle. We have to be perfectly prepared to let go of any thought, opinion, or inclination if logical thinking demands it. Certainty in the higher worlds cannot be attained if one is in any way attached to one's own opinions.

"All prejudices must fall from you" is inscribed over the door leading to the second trial, and "Without healthy human understanding all steps are in vain" stands at the entrance to the first. This by no means implies that esoteric students lose the poetry of life and the capacity for enthusiasm.

Once we have matured sufficiently along these lines, a third trial awaits us. This trial is without any tangible, distinct goal. Everything is up to us. We find ourselves in a situation where nothing moves us to act. We must each find our own way, by ourselves and out of ourselves. There are no things or people who might help us to act. Nothing and nobody can give us the strength we need, except we ourselves. If we do not find this strength within ourselves, we will soon be back where we were before.

We must courageously overcome all that keeps us from listening to the spirit. What matters is that we show presence of mind under these circumstances.

Everyday life can serve as an esoteric school for spiritual presence of mind, just as it does for the other qualities required for initiation. This is particularly true in the case of those who, suddenly confronted with life tasks or problems, have learned to act rapidly and decisively, without hesitation or reflection. We learn this ability above all in situations whose successful outcome depends upon speedy action. For example, if we can act quickly when a misfortune threatens—one that could not be averted if we hesitated even for a moment—and if we can make such decisiveness a permanent quality, we have already unconsciously prepared ourselves for the third "trial." This trial is intended to develop absolute presence of mind.

In schools for esoteric training, this trial is called the Air Trial. Here we can rely neither on the solid ground of outer motivation, nor on insights gained from the shapes, colors, and so on, we came to know in the stages of preparation and illumination. Instead, we must now rely completely upon ourselves.

> 16. *Looking back at what has been shared regarding the trials, please share a few thoughts on the following questions:*
>
> 1. *Has life brought you any challenges/trials that resemble the ones described above? If so, please name them and identify what type of trial you think you experienced in each instance.*
> 2. *Why do you think trials like these are important for self-development?*

When we are sufficiently matured for these experiences, we receive what is called symbolically the "potion of oblivion." That is, we are initiated into the secret of action uninterrupted by the lower memory. This is necessary for an initiate, who must always have complete confidence in the immediate present. We must know how to tear down the veils of memory that surround us at every moment of our lives. Otherwise, if I judge today's experiences by those of yesterday, I become subject to many errors. This does not mean that we should deny our prior experiences. On the contrary, as far as possible, they should always be present. But initiates have to be able to judge each new experience on its own merits and let it work upon them, untroubled by the past.

In other words, I must always be ready to receive a new revelation from each and every being and thing. To judge the new on the basis of the old only leads to errors. Yet the memory of past experiences is useful precisely because it enables one to see new ones. That is, without a given past experience I might never see the characteristic feature of the things or beings I encounter. Past experiences should help us to see what is new, not to judge it. As initiates we develop quite specific faculties for this. Thereby many things reveal themselves that remain hidden from the uninitiated.

The second potion given to initiates is the "potion of memory." This enables one to keep the higher mysteries always present and in mind. Our ordinary memory is insufficient for this. We must become completely one with the higher mysteries. Merely knowing them is not enough. They must become as much a matter of course to us in our daily actions as eating and drinking are to ordinary people. They must become practice, habit, disposition, so that we do not need to think about them in the ordinary sense.

17. What is the value of forgetting?
What is the value of remembering?

4. Practical Considerations

The present chapter will examine in greater detail some practical approaches to esoteric development that are part of the higher education of soul and spirit. These practices are such that basically any of us can adopt them, regardless of any other rules we are following. Indeed, anyone who follows these additional suggestions will advance quite far in esoteric science.

We must strive especially to train our capacity for patience. Every stirring of impatience paralyzes, even destroys, the higher faculties latent within us. We should not desire or expect to achieve boundless insights into the higher worlds overnight, for then as a rule they will certainly not come to us. Instead, contentment with even our smallest achievement, along with calm and detachment, should increasingly fill our souls.

18. Why is it so hard to be patient is a world of "just Google it"?

"I must do everything I can for the education of my soul and spirit; but I will wait calmly until the higher powers consider me worthy of illumination." Once when this thought has become so powerful in us that it has become part of our character, then we are on the right path.

Before long, this new character trait puts its outward signature upon us. Our gaze becomes calm, our eye steady, our movements confident, our decisions definite. Any nervousness we previously felt gradually disappears. At this point, certain apparently insignificant little "rules" must be observed. For example, let us say someone offends us. Previously, before esoteric training, we would have turned our feelings against the offender. Irritation and anger would have bubbled up within us.

Now that we are on the path to higher knowledge, however, the thought immediately comes to us: "This insult does not alter my true worth." Then we do what needs to be done, calmly and with detachment rather than out of anger. This does not mean that we simply swallow insults; rather, we should be as calm and confident in responding to insults directed at us as we would be if we acted on behalf of someone else who had been insulted.

Patience has the effect of attracting the treasures of higher knowledge. Impatience repels them. Haste and unrest achieve nothing in the higher realms of existence.

Above all, longing and craving must be silenced. These are soul qualities in the face of which all higher knowledge shyly retreats.

We must look our own mistakes, weaknesses, and shortcomings in the eye with inner truthfulness. Each time we find an excuse for a weakness, we place an obstacle before us on our upward path. Such obstacles can be removed only by becoming enlightened about ourselves. There is but one way to overcome failings and weaknesses—to see them for what they are, with inner truthfulness.

Such self-knowledge, of course, is difficult. The temptation to deceive oneself is enormous. But if we make a habit of being honest with ourselves, the doors to greater insight open for us.

> 19. If one looks in the mirror in the morning, one sees what is there. Yet looking at our "mistakes, weaknesses, shortcomings" with inner truthfulness is not so easy. Why?

Esoteric development requires, above all, the education of our life of wishes and aspirations. This does not mean that we should have no wishes or desires. If we are to attain something, we must first wish for it. And our wishes will always find fulfillment if a special kind of force lies behind them. This force or power arises from right knowledge. "Do not aspire to something until you know what is right in a given domain."

Whenever I am angry or irritated, I build a wall around me in the soul world and the forces that should develop the eyes of my soul cannot approach me.

The gift of seeing arises only when we have suppressed all the traits hindering the emergence of the latent faculties corresponding to them.

In addition to anger and irritation, we must also struggle against other traits, such as fearfulness, superstition, prejudice, vanity, ambition, curiosity, the urge to gossip, and the tendency to discriminate on the basis of such outer characteristics as social status, gender, race, and so on.

We place an obstacle in the path of our esoteric development whenever we say something without first having carefully refined and purified it in our thoughts. This can best be made clear by an example: If someone says something to me that I must respond to, I must make an effort to pay more attention to the other person's beliefs, feelings, and even prejudices than to anything I myself might add to the conversation at that moment. In other words, if one is on an esoteric path one must dedicate oneself conscientiously to schooling an impeccable sense of tact or delicacy.

"It does not matter if what I think differs from what the other person thinks. What matters is that, as a result of what I can contribute to the conversation, the other discovers what is right out of themselves."

As we develop gentleness, another trait begins to form in our souls: quiet attention to all the subtleties of soul life surrounding us, together with the utter stillness of our own soul's activity. If we achieve this, then what is taking place in the soul life around us helps our own soul unfold and grow organically, just as sunlight helps plants to flourish. Thus, patient gentleness and stillness open the soul to the world of souls and our spirit to the country of spirits.

Become perfectly still and inwardly silent. And wait patiently for the higher worlds to fashion the eyes and ears of your soul.

Nevertheless, whatever our circumstances, it is good to practice the exercises whenever possible in the quiet peacefulness, inner dignity, and charm of nature.

The ideal situation would be to pursue our esoteric training among green plants and sunny mountains, surrounded by the loveliness of nature's simplicity.

If we cannot see the forests turning green day by day each spring, we should at least nourish our hearts with the lofty teachings of the Bhagavad Gita, the Gospel of St. John, and Thomas à Kempis, and with the findings of Spiritual Science.

20. Have you ever had a special place (at the foot of a tree, in a glade, on a rocking chair, or on a boulder on top of a mountain, for instance) where you could practice contemplation? If so, where was it? If not, what place would you choose and why?

5. Requirements for Esoteric Training

What follows is a description of the series of conditions to be met by the student. It should be noted that none of these requires complete perfection; we need only strive toward that goal. No one can fulfill these conditions completely, but everyone can set out on the path to their fulfillment. It is our attitude and our will to begin that are important.

The first requirement is that we turn our attention to the improvement of our physical and mental or spiritual health. Our health does not in the first place depend on us. Yet we can make an effort to improve it. Sound understanding—healthy cognition—occurs only in a healthy human being.

We should strive to take care of ourselves.

With regard to physical health, warding off harmful influences is more important than anything else. To fulfill our obligations, we often have to do things that are not conducive to our health. Indeed, in certain cases we must learn to place responsibility above health. Yet there is much that we can give up, if only we have the good will to do so! Certainly, duty is often more important than health and sometimes even than life itself. Gratification, however, should never be the first priority. For the student of the esoteric way, pleasure should be only a means to health and life. Here we must be completely honest and truthful with ourselves. It is no use leading an ascetic life, if this arises out of the same motives of gratification, as do other pleasures.

Therefore, it is especially important for a student to strive for complete mental and spiritual health. An unhealthy inner life impedes our access to higher knowledge. Clear, calm thinking, and reliable sensations and feelings are essential. Nothing should

32

be further from us than any tendency toward fantasy, excitability, nervousness, inflation, and fanaticism. We must acquire a sound eye for all that life presents to us. We must learn to cope confidently with life. We must learn to allow things to speak to us quietly, letting them work upon us.

> 21. *In the last few years, how have you tried to ward off harmful influences and take care of yourself? What aspects do you struggle with most?*

The second requirement is that we feel ourselves to be a part of the whole of life.

This kind of attitude will gradually change our whole way of thinking—about the greatest as well as the least of things. For example, I will look upon criminals differently. I will now withhold my judgment and contemplate our common humanity, thinking: "I am a human being just as this person is. Perhaps it was only my upbringing, which my situation in life has given me, that spared me this fate." Then I will reflect that criminals, who are my brothers and sisters in humanity, might have turned out very differently had they received the attention and encouragement my mentors gave me. I will be led to reflect that I have received something that was withheld from them—that my good fortune comes at their expense.

It is then but a small step to the insight that, as a member or organ of humanity as a whole, I am jointly responsible, with all human beings, for everything that happens.

It would therefore be quite wrong to connect the demands of esoteric schooling with any external demand for reform or even political change. The education of the spirit has nothing to do with such things. Political activists generally know what to ask of other people, but they hardly ever talk about asking anything of themselves.

22. If possible, go on the website anthroposophy.org and look for information on the "prison outreach program." Even if you have limited time, read a few of the letters, some from death row, and look at the artwork. Both are inspired by prisoners who have been reading on Anthroposophy. What do you think of their responses?

The third requirement of esoteric training is intimately connected to the second. It requires that we win through to the conviction that thoughts and feelings are as important for the world as actions. We should recognize that when we hate our fellow human beings it is just as destructive as when we physically strike them.

We must know that what we feel has as much impact upon the world as the work done by our hands.

With this, the fourth requirement is already stated. We must acquire the conviction that our true nature does not lie without but within. We can achieve nothing spiritually if we regard ourselves merely as a product, a result, of the physical world. The very basis of esoteric training is feeling that we are soul-spiritual beings. Once we have made this feeling our own, we are ready to distinguish between our inner sense of duty and outer success.

Only the inner voice of the soul, as it honestly strives for higher knowledge, can confirm our truths. Yet we must also learn as much as possible about our environment and find out what is useful and good for it. And, if we do so, we will develop within ourselves what esoteric science calls "the spiritual scales" or the "balance"—on one of whose trays lies a helpful heart, open to the needs of the world, and on the other, inner firmness and unshakable endurance.

23. Are you aware of when "the spiritual scales" tip too far one way or the other? Why does that happen?

This brings us to the fifth requirement: steadfastness in following through on a resolution once it has been made. Nothing should lead us to abandon something we have decided upon except the insight that we have made a mistake. Each resolution we make is a force that works in its own way—even when it is not immediately successful in the area where it is first applied. Success is crucial only when we act out of longing. But any action motivated by craving is worthless from the point of view of the higher world. In the higher world, love is the only motivation for action.

The sixth requirement is that we develop the feeling of gratitude for all that we receive. We should know that our very existence is a gift from the whole universe. How much is necessary for human beings to receive and sustain their existence! We owe so much to nature and to other people. Grateful thoughts such as these must become second nature for those engaged in esoteric training.

Only if I love something can it reveal itself to me. And every revelation should fill me with thankfulness, for I am made richer by it.

> 24. *Make a short list of the things you are most grateful for: people, events, experiences that have helped you thus far on your life journey.*

All the above conditions come together in the seventh: always to understand life as these conditions demand.

Everything in our inner life must develop through something outward. Just as a painting that is still only in the painter's head cannot be said really to exist, so esoteric training cannot be said to exist if there is no outward expression of it. Once we know that the outer must express the inner, we can no longer hold the strict forms in low regard. It is true that the spirit is more important than the form—which indeed is nothing at all without the spirit—but the spirit would remain idle if it did not create a form for itself.

To believe in and love humanity is the basis of all striving for the truth. Our striving must be built upon trust and love for humanity—although it does not begin there. Rather, it must flow out of the soul's own forces. And this love for humanity must gradually expand into love for all beings, and indeed for all existence.

> 25. Can you name a few famous people whom you think demon-
> strated extraordinary love of humanity and striving for truth?

The best way to combat wickedness and imperfection is to create what is good and whole. We cannot create something out of nothing, but we can transform what is incomplete into something more perfect. The more we strengthen our creative tendencies, the sooner we will find ourselves capable of the right attitude toward whatever is bad and imperfect.

Anyone who enters esoteric training must realize that its purpose is to build up, not tear down. Therefore, we should bring to it a desire to work sincerely and devotedly, not to criticize and destroy. We should become capable of reverence because we are to learn things we do not yet know. We should look reverently toward what opens before us. Work and reverence are the fundamental attitudes expected of us as esoteric students.

Esoteric training, however, depends on learning. As esoteric students, our willingness to learn should be unconditional. It is far better to withhold our judgment on something we do not understand than to condemn it. We can leave understanding until later.

The more levels of cognition we attain, the more we need to be able to listen attentively, calmly, and reverently.

6. EFFECTS OF INITIATION

We [now] direct our care and attention to eight specific soul processes that we usually perform without care or attention.

1. The first soul process concerns the way in which we acquire ideas or mental images. As a rule, we leave this to chance. We happen to see or hear something, and then we form our concepts on that basis.... We must guide our conceptual life to become a true mirror of the outer world. All our striving must be to eliminate false ideas from the soul.

2. The second soul process to be considered—much in the same way as the first—is how we make decisions. Any decision, even the most trivial, should be made only after thorough, well-reasoned deliberation. We should remove all thoughtless activity and meaningless action from our souls. We must have well-thought-out reasons for all we do. Anything we cannot find a reason for, we must refrain from doing.

3. The third soul process concerns speech. When we are esoteric students, every word should have substance and meaning. Talk for talking's sake diverts us from the path. We should talk neither too much nor too little.

4. The fourth soul process concerns the ordering of our outer actions. As esoteric students, we should try to manage our affairs so that they fit both with the affairs of others and with events around us. We should abstain from any behavior that would disturb others or otherwise go against what is happening around us.

5. At this point, the fifth soul process comes under consideration, namely, the arrangement and organization of our life as a whole. As esoteric students, we must strive to live in harmony

37

with both nature and spirit. We must be neither overhasty, nor slow and lazy. Hyperactivity and laxity should be equally alien to us.

6. The sixth soul process has to do with human striving or effort. As esoteric students we must assess our talents and abilities and then act in accordance with this self-knowledge. We should not try to do anything that lies beyond our powers, yet we must always do everything that lies within our powers to do.

7. The seventh soul process involves the effort to learn as much as possible from life. As esoteric students, nothing comes to us in life that does not provide an opportunity to gather experiences useful for the future. Mistakes and imperfections become an incentive to perform more correctly and perfectly whenever a similar situation next arises. In the same way, we can learn from watching others. We should try to gather as rich a treasure of experience as possible, conscientiously drawing on it for advice at all times. We should do nothing without looking back upon the experiences that can help us to decide and act.

8. Finally, the eighth soul process: as esoteric students, we should periodically turn and look inward. We must sink absorbed into ourselves, gently taking counsel with ourselves, shaping and testing our basic principles of life, mentally reviewing what we know, weighing our obligations, pondering the meaning and purpose of life, and so forth.

26. Reviewing the previous eight steps, which ones do you find to be the most challenging? Which ones come more easily for you? Give a few examples of each.

Truthfulness, sincerity, and honesty are constructive forces, while lying, falsity, and insincerity are destructive ones. On the esoteric path, we must be aware that what matters is not "good intentions," but what we actually do. If I think or say something that does not correspond to reality, I destroy something in my spiritual sense organ, regardless of how good I think my intentions are.

Such tact, precision, and delicacy in forming and expressing judgments must gradually become our signature as esoteric students.

27. Here are six exercises to practice. Adopt one for a day or even a week and see how you do. Then move on to the next. Write a one-sentence review of how you did with each one.

1. *First, we pay attention to directing the sequence of our thoughts—this is the so-called practice of the control of thoughts.*

2. *Second, we must bring an equally logical consistency into our actions—this is the practice of the control of actions.*

3. *Third, we must cultivate perseverance.*

4. *Fourth, we must develop forbearance (or tolerance) toward other people, other beings, and events.*

5. *Fifth, we must develop openness and impartiality toward all the phenomena of life.*

6. *Sixth, we must achieve a certain balance in life (or serenity).*

7. CHANGES IN THE DREAM LIFE OF THE ESOTERIC STUDENT

An indication that we have reached, or soon will reach, the stage of development described in the last chapter is the change that occurs in our dream life. Previously, our dreams were muddled and random. Now they begin to take on a more orderly character. Their images connect in a meaningful way, like the thoughts and ideas of waking consciousness. We begin to recognize lawfulness, and cause and effect in them.

At the same time, the content of our dreams also changes. Whereas our dreams formerly contained only echoes of our daily lives, and transformed impressions of our surroundings or our own bodily condition, the images we now see arise out of a world unknown to us before. At first, however, the general character of the dreams remains the same. That is, compared to waking consciousness, our dreams continue to express their content symbolically. Any careful study of dreams confirms this undeniably symbolic character. For example, we may dream that we have caught a horrible creature that feels unpleasant in our hands. Awakening, we find we have been clutching a corner of the blanket. The dream expresses this experience—not directly and unvarnished, but in a symbol.

Or we may dream that we are fleeing a pursuer and feel afraid. Waking up, we discover that we suffered palpitations of the heart while we were asleep. Again, if our stomach is filled with heavy, difficult-to-digest food when we fall asleep, this too can produce anxious dreams. Events occurring in our surroundings while we are asleep may similarly be reflected symbolically in dreams. The striking of a clock can evoke images of soldiers marching by to the beat of drums. Or the crash of a chair falling can stimulate a whole drama, in which the noise is symbolically reflected in the dream as a gunshot.

The more orderly and structured dreams that we begin to experience once our ether bodies have begun to develop retain this symbolic mode of expression, but they no longer reflect only events that are connected to our physical surroundings or bodily processes. For, as the dreams originating in physical reality become increasingly regulated, they begin to mix with images expressing conditions and events of another world. At this point, then, we begin to have experiences inaccessible to ordinary waking consciousness.

When dreaming we are actually in a different world from the one revealed to us by the physical senses. However, as long as our spiritual organs are undeveloped, we can form only a muddled idea of this world. Until then it exists for us only as much as the sensible world would exist for a being with only the most primitive, rudimentary eyes.

We cannot perceive anything with them in our waking state because the impressions made upon them in that state are very weak. The reason for this is similar to why we do not see the stars by day. Namely, their light is too weak when compared with the powerful light of the Sun. In the same way, the weaker impressions of the spiritual world count for very little when compared to the powerful impressions of the physical senses.

When the doors of the outer senses are closed during sleep, these impressions from the spiritual world light up at random. As they do so we then become, as dreamers, aware of experiences in the other world. This marks the beginning of our contact and communication with a new world.

We must now accomplish—by means of the instructions provided by esoteric training—a twofold task. First, we must become as conscious of what we observe in our dreams as we are of what we observe in waking life. Second, once we can do this, we must be able to carry this consciousness of dream observations into our ordinary waking state. In other words, our attention for spiritual impressions must be so developed that these impressions no longer vanish in the presence of physical impressions. Rather, we must be able to have both types of perceptions at the same time, side by side.

28. Please take a few minutes each morning to try and recall your dreams. If you can, jot down a few things in a "sleep journal." After one or two weeks, look back at what you have written. Have you become more aware of your dreams?

Next, we must "grow" into this higher self. That is, we must consider it a real being and behave accordingly. This means that we immerse ourselves more and more in the idea and living feeling that our physical body and what we used to call our "self" are really only instruments of the higher "I." In this way we begin to develop a relationship to our lower self that is like the relationship those who live only in the sense world feel toward their tools and vehicles. Just as we do not think of the car we drive as part of our "I"-being, even though we may say, "I drive" or "I travel," so the words "I go in through the door" now come to mean, for those who have developed themselves, "I take my body in through the door."

This idea must become so natural and obvious to us that we never for a moment lose our solid footing in physical reality. We must never allow any feeling of estrangement or alienation from the sense world to arise.

As spiritually developed persons, however, we now feel ourselves as if "united" with the spiritual objects we perceive, as if we were "inside" them. In other words, we wander from place to place in spiritual space. For this reason, Spiritual Science calls those at this level of inner development "Wanderers," for they are not yet at home anywhere.

Were we to remain mere "wanderers," however, we would find it impossible ever to truly define any object in spiritual space. Indeed, just as we define objects and places in physical space by starting from a given point of reference, so likewise if we wish to define things in spiritual space we must establish a similar reference point from which to begin. We must find a place in this other world, explore it thoroughly, and spiritually take possession of it. We must establish our spiritual homeland in this place, and then set everything else in relation to it. This is just what we do in the physical world. There, too, we view things from the perspective of the ideas and beliefs of our native country. A Berliner, for example, will describe London in a different way than a New Yorker will.

Yet there is a great difference between our physical and our spiritual homeland. We have nothing to do with the place of our physical birth, where we grow up and instinctively absorb various ideas and beliefs, which then involuntarily color everything we experience. Our spiritual home place is different. We create a spiritual home for ourselves in full consciousness. Therefore, any judgment emanating from it is made in perfect, lucid freedom. In the language of Spiritual Science, this making of a spiritual home is called "Building a Hut."

8. ACHIEVING CONTINUITY OF CONSCIOUSNESS

Human life unfolds in three alternating states. These are the waking state; the state of dream sleep; and the state of deep, dreamless sleep. To better understand how a person may attain deeper insights into the spiritual worlds, we must therefore form some idea of the changes that occur—for those seeking such knowledge—in each of these states.

Normally, we consider such dreams as simply a particular manifestation of sleep, and hence generally distinguish only two states of consciousness: sleeping and waking. In esoteric science, however, the dream state has a separate significance, independent of the two other states.

As we evolve further, this new dream-born world not only becomes the equal of outer sensory reality with regard to inner truth, but also reveals facts depicting, in the full sense of the word, a higher reality.

We evolve inwardly to the point of being able to transfer into waking consciousness the state we first formed out of our dream life. This enriches the sense world with something quite new. It is as if we were born blind and were to undergo a successful operation: we would find the world enriched by what our eyes then saw. It is the same when we become clairvoyant in the manner described above: we see the whole surrounding world filled with new qualities, new things, new beings, and so forth. Then we need no longer wait for dreams to live in another world. Now we can transpose ourselves into the state for higher perception whenever it is appropriate. In fact, this state now becomes as important to us as our active perceptions are in ordinary life when compared to what we perceive passively. Thus, it may truly be said that, as students of the esoteric, we open the sense organs of the soul and behold things that must remain hidden from the physical senses.

To describe these experiences is not easy. Our languages were designed for the material world and contain words that only approximate things not belonging to this world. Nevertheless, for the time being, we must use words to describe the higher worlds. But we can do so only if we make free use of analogy in much of what we say. We can do this because everything in the universe is related to everything else. Indeed, the things and beings of the higher and material worlds are sufficiently related so that—with a little good will—we can obtain a conception of the higher worlds through words intended for the material world. But we must always be conscious of the fact that a great part of such descriptions of the suprasensory worlds must inevitably consist of analogies and symbols.

The conscious—and, at first, isolated—experiences that emerge from the ocean of unconsciousness in deep sleep are best understood as a kind of "hearing." One may describe them as perceptible tones and words. Just as in comparison to ordinary sense experience we may describe what happens in dream sleep as a kind of "seeing," so we may compare what occurs in deep sleep to impressions received by the ears.

Once we notice such deep sleep experiences, our main task is to make them as clear and vivid as possible. At first this will be very difficult, for we have only an extremely faint experience of what we perceive during this state. Thus, upon awakening, we may know that we have had certain experiences, but what these were remains still quite unclear. The most important thing at this early stage is to remain calm and composed. We must never for a moment yield to impatience and restlessness, for these are always harmful.

Once this faculty for perception in sleep has been achieved, and sleep experiences stand before our consciousness in complete clarity and vividness, we can then focus our attention on them. We shall find that we are able to distinguish, with some precision, two kinds of experiences. The first is completely different from anything we have ever known. Initially it delights and uplifts us, but for the moment we should leave it alone. Such experiences, in fact, are the first heralds of a higher spiritual world in which we find our bearings only later. Attentive observation of the second kind of experiences reveals a certain relationship between these and the ordinary world we live in. We find that these experiences illuminate not only our daily reflections but also the things around us that we have tried to grasp with our ordinary mind but could not.

We feel increasingly as though a higher world were softly whispering in our ears answers to the riddles we ponder. We find ourselves able to connect with our everyday life what we receive from the higher world in sleep. Things that we could only think about before now become as vivid and meaningful to us as any sensory experience in the physical world.

> 29. Have you ever had the experience of an inner voice "softly whispering" into your ears something that concerns a life mystery, something you have been pondering? Socrates called this voice the "daemon"; during the Middle Ages, it was called your "angel." Some call it one's "higher self." Do you have any basis of experience that affirms such inner "whispering"?

It is easy to see that, just as our physical senses are useful for the accurate observation of the world only if they are properly developed and structured, so this higher capacity of perception can benefit us only if the soul's newly opened organs of perception are in good order. As indicated above, it is we ourselves who produce these higher senses by practicing the exercises that are part of our esoteric schooling. These exercises, of course, consist of concentration and meditation. Concentration means that we focus our attention on particular mental pictures and concepts connected with the mysteries of the cosmos. Meditation means living in such ideas, immersing ourselves in them in accordance with the instructions. Through such concentration and meditation we work on the soul and develop its organs of perception. Applying ourselves to the tasks of concentration and meditation, we help the soul to grow within the body, just as an embryo does within the mother's womb. The appearance of the isolated experiences that occur in sleep (as described above) signals the approach of the moment of birth for the soul that has now become free—for by this whole process the soul has literally become a different being, one we have germinated and brought to maturity within ourselves.

In sleep, however, when the body and its activities based on sense perception are at rest, the activity of the higher soul, at first so delicate and inconspicuous, can make itself felt. In other words, we find ourselves experiencing, by means of the force of the spiritual world we have now entered, as well as by our continuing practice of the appropriate exercises, an ever-expanding extension of consciousness in periods of deep sleep. More and more experiences emerge from unconsciousness, our periods of unconscious sleep grow shorter and shorter, and gradually these isolated experiences come together of their own accord, without their real connection being in any way disturbed by such conjectures and conclusions as could derive only from the ordinary mind accustomed to the sensory world.

As we follow these guidelines, we draw ever nearer to that stage on the path to higher knowledge at which we can transform previously unconscious states of sleep life into full consciousness.

Esoteric, or occult, science calls the important stage of development, wherein we become conscious in sleep, "continuity (or unbrokenness) of consciousness."

30. How might such an extension of consciousness be helpful in living a more complete, fulfilling life?

2

Overcoming Nervousness: Nervousness and "I"-ness

Rudolf Steiner, Munich, January 11, 1912

The suggestions to be given today connect with much that we already know, but they can still be useful for one or another of us, and can even lead us into a more exact contemplation of the essence of the human being and of its connection with the world. The anthroposophist can very often hear all kinds of things from non-anthroposophists, apart from the many rebuttals and objections against Spiritual Science lately mentioned in the public lectures. For example, both learned and unlearned people object over and over again to our speaking, in Spiritual Science, about the division of the whole human being into those four members that we always bring up: physical body, ether—or life—body, astral body, and the "I." Then doubters can object, so to speak: Well, maybe that's how it is for someone who has developed certain hidden forces of the soul; maybe such a person can see this composition of the human being; but someone who doesn't see such things can have no reason to turn toward such a viewpoint. However, we must emphasize that, if one is attentive to human life, this life in a certain sense can give corroborations of what spirit-knowledge has to say. Further, if one applies what one can learn from spirit knowledge to one's life, then such an application proves extraordinarily useful. One soon finds that this usefulness (I don't mean here usefulness in a low sense, but usefulness that is of use for life in the most beautiful sense) can gradually give us a kind of conviction, even if we do not want to enter into what clairvoyant perception offers.

It is only too well known that in our time people complain often of what we can encompass with the much-feared word *nervousness*. And we would not be surprised in the least if someone feels driven to say: In our time, there is really no one left who is not nervous about something. How understandable this statement is, in a certain way! Quite apart from the social relationships and conditions to which we can ascribe this or that cause for such nervousness, the nervous conditions, as we have described them, are present. They express themselves in life in the most varied ways; they express themselves, as we could perhaps say, in the lightest way, in the least uncomfortable way, when a person becomes what we could call a will-o'-the-wisp of the soul. This is the name I would give to someone who is incapable of holding onto a thought properly and pursuing its consequences in a real way. Such people hop from one thought to another; if you want to hold them in one place they have already long ago gone somewhere else. A hastiness of the soul life—this is often the lightest form of nervousness.

Another kind of nervousness is that of people who don't know what to do with themselves; when things require a decision from them they cannot decide, and never really know for sure what they should do in this or that situation.

And then these conditions can lead on to other, already more serious cases, such that this nervousness lives itself out gradually more and more in actual forms of disease, for which, perhaps, one can cite no organic cause. These forms of disease sometimes mimic organic diseases in a deceptive way, so that one could believe the person has, perhaps, a serious stomach ailment, but really suffers only from what one can sum up, even if trivially and without much meaning, under the word *nervousness*. And countless other conditions: who among us is not familiar with them? Who does not suffer from them, either because we have them ourselves or because others in our environment have them? One need not go so far as to speak about the great events of outer life as a "political addiction," but people have spoken recently about that kind of nervous activity in public life as a kind of conduct that otherwise only expresses itself in an individual who has been infected by a kind of "alcoholism." The word is appropriate for the way political affairs have been conducted in Europe over recent months. One also sees in outer life something about which one could say, here, too, one notices not only that nervousness is present, but people sense it in a certain connection as something quite unpleasant. Everywhere, then, something akin to nervousness is present.

All this will, in the near future, grow worse and worse for people. If people remain as they are, then a good outlook for the future cannot by any means be offered. For there are harmful influences that affect our current life in a quite extraordinary way and that carry over from one person to the other like an epidemic. Therefore, people become a bit diseased in this direction: not only the ones who have the illness, but also others, who are perhaps only weak but otherwise healthy, get it by a kind of infection.

It is enormously harmful for our time that a great number of the people who arrive in prominent public positions study in the way that people study at present. There are actually whole branches of study in which one lives, let us say, the whole year at the university doing things other than thinking through and studying through what the professors are saying; one goes into lectures now and then, but what one really wants to learn is acquired in a few weeks—that is to say, people cram. The bad part is the cramming. Since, in a certain regard, this cramming goes as far as to the lower grades, the ills that come from it are by no means inconsiderable. The essential part of this cramming is that there is no real connection of the soul-interest, of the inner-most kernel of being, with what one crams. In the schools, the reigning opinion among the students is even: Oh, if only I could now forget what I have just learned! So that vehement wanting to possess what one learns is not present. A slight chain of interest links the human soul kernel with what people take in.

Now people can be made fit in this way, in a certain regard, to take a hand in public life, because they crammed, or learned, the thing they wanted to learn, but since they are not inwardly connected with it, they are far away in the soul from what they are doing with their head. And for the whole human being there is hardly anything worse than being far away in the soul, with one's heart, from what the head must perform. This not only goes against the nature of a finer, more sensitive person, but also influences the strength and energy of the human etheric body to the highest degree—precisely of the etheric body. The ether, or life, body becomes ever weaker from such activity, because of the slight connection that exists between the human soul kernel and what the person is doing. The more people have to do what does not interest them, the weaker they make their ether body.

Anthroposophy, if acquired in a healthy way, should do more than teach people that human beings consist of a physical body, an ether body, and so forth; Anthroposophy should also have the healthy effect of developing these individual members strongly within the human being.

Now, if we make a very simple experiment, but repeat this experiment eagerly, then a triviality can actually work wonders. Forgive me if I speak today just of individual observations, or trivialities, but these can become very significant for human life. The light forgetfulness that people sometimes show is intimately connected with what I have just described. Light forgetfulness is something unpleasant in life; Anthroposophy can, however, show us that this forgetfulness is damaging to health in the most eminent sense. And, strange as it may sound, it is true that many outbreaks of human nature that border on being very diseased would be avoided if people were less forgetful. Now, you can say, they are forgetful; indeed, who can say (as we realize when we have an overview of life) that they are completely free of forgetfulness? Take a truly trivial case: we may discover that we are forgetful, in that we never know where we have put the things we use. Isn't this something that happens in life? One person cannot find the cufflinks placed somewhere the evening before, another can never find one's pencil, and so on. It seems strange and banal to talk about such matters, but they happen in life. And precisely from observation of what we can learn in Anthroposophy, there is a good exercise for gradually improving this condition of forgetfulness.

Here is the very simple technique: now let us assume a lady puts down, say, her brooch or a man puts down his cufflinks somewhere in the evening, and, when they cannot find these objects the next morning, they realize their tendency to forgetfulness. Now you could say, yes, certainly, and one can accustom oneself to always putting them down in the same place. That won't be possible for all objects. However, we do not want to speak at the moment of this particular means of curing oneself, but rather of a much more effective means. In other words, assume that a person who notices a tendency to forgetfulness immediately says inwardly, I now want to put the objects in very different places, but I want never to place an object in a specific spot without also developing this thought when I put it there: I have placed this object in this spot! Then one tries to imprint in oneself an image of the surroundings. Let us assume we place a safety pin at the edge of a table at the corner. We lay it down with the thought: I am laying down this pin on this edge and I imprint the right angle around it as a picture, such that the pin is surrounded on two sides by edges, and so on, and I go calmly away from the place. I will see that, even if it doesn't work out right away in every case, if I make this practice a rule then my forgetfulness will gradually fall away from me. It depends on a very specific thought being formulated, namely the thought: I am laying the pin down there. I have connected my "I" with what I am doing, and in addition I have added something in the way of a picture—imagery in the thought of what I am doing and, in addition to this pictorial mental imaging, bringing the fact into connection with the kernel of my essence. This bringing together with the soul-spiritual kernel of essence, as addressed with the little word "*I,*" along with imagery can sharpen our memory quite fundamentally. In this way we have something useful for life, since we become less forgetful. Perhaps we would not make so much of it if that were all that could be achieved. However, much more can be achieved in this way.

Let us assume that it became a custom among people to evoke such thoughts when they lay down certain objects—then this custom alone would evoke a strengthening of the human ether body. The human ether body is in fact more and more consolidated by doing this kind of thing; it becomes ever stronger and stronger. We have learned from Anthroposophy that the ether, or life, body must be for us in a certain sense the bearer of the memory. If we do something that strengthens the powers of memory, then we can understand right away that such a strengthening of the powers of memory aids our ether body. As anthroposophists we need not be so very surprised about it. But suppose you suggest to someone who not only is forgetful, but also shows certain conditions of nervousness, what has been described here. If the restless or nervous person does this— accompanies the placement of objects with such thoughts—then you will see that he or she not only becomes less forgetful, but also gradually, through the strengthening of the ether body, puts aside certain so-called nervous conditions. Then a proof will have been provided, through life, that what we say about the ether body is right. For if we behave in the corresponding way toward the ether body, it definitely shows that it assumes these forces; so what we say about it is correct. Life proves, in such a case, that this is extraordinarily important.

Another matter, which once again can seem to be a triviality, but which is extraordinarily important! You know that what we can call the physical body and the ether body border immediately on one another in the human being. The ether body is immediately contained within the physical. Now, today, you can make an observation that is not so very rare at all, an observation whose validity is not known to those people about whom we make the observation. When we make this observation and bear within us a healthy, compassionate soul, then we will have, precisely, compassion for these people we are observing. Have you seen, for example, people writing at the post office counter who make very peculiar movements before they begin to write a letter—before they begin to write a B, for instance. First they make some movements in the air and then begin! Or it need not even go so far; for this is already the indication of a serious condition, if people are forced through their jobs to do such things; it may merely go so far that the people—watch them sometime—have to give themselves a little jolt, so to speak, with each stroke, and in fact they write jaggedly, not going up and down evenly, but jaggedly. You can see it in the handwriting in this way.

From spiritual scientific knowledge we can understand such a condition in the following way: For a completely healthy human being—healthy in regard to the physical body and ether body—the ether body, which is directed by the astral body, must always be able to take absolute hold of the physical body, and the physical body must everywhere, in all its movements, be able to become a servant of the ether body. If the physical body moves on its own, beyond what the soul can really want—that is, what the astral body can really want—then it is an unhealthy condition, a preponderance of the physical body over the etheric body. And in everyone who has the conditions just described, we once again have to do with a weakness of the etheric body, which consists in its no longer being able fully to control the physical body. This relationship of the etheric body to the physical body even lies, esoterically, at the base of all conditions of cramping, which are fundamentally connected in that the etheric body exercises a lesser command over the physical body than it should exercise, so that the physical dominates and carries out all kinds of movements on its own. Meanwhile, the human being is healthy in relation to the fullness of its being only if everything that it does is subordinate to the will of the astral body.

Now here again there is a possibility, if this condition has not gained too much the upper hand, of helping people: only one must reckon with the esoteric facts. One has to reckon with the need for the etheric body as such to be strengthened. One must to a certain extent believe in the existence and effective capacity of the ether body. Suppose an unfortunate man has so ruined himself that he continually makes restless motions with his fingers before he begins to write this or that letter. Now it will be good in all circumstances to advise the person: All right, take a vacation and write less for a while and you will get better! But this advice is only a halfway advice; one could do much more if one also gave the person another suggestion, the second half of the advice: And try, without making a lot of effort—a quarter or a half hour every day are enough—try to take on a different handwriting, to change your writing style, so that you are required not to write mechanically, as you have up until now, but to pay attention! Whereas you used to write the *F* in that way, now write it steeper and in a quite different form, so that you must pay attention! Accustom yourself to painting the letters.

If spiritual knowledge were more widespread, then when such a person came back from vacation and had acquired a new handwriting style, his superiors would not say, "What kind of nutty guy are you, you write completely differently!" People would realize that this is a fundamental curative technique. We are forced, when we change our writing in this way, to be attentive to what we are doing, and to be attentive to what we are doing always means to bring the innermost kernel of our being into intimate connection with the matter at hand. Everything, in turn, that brings the innermost kernel of our being into connection with what we do strengthens our ether body. In this way we become healthy human beings. It would be good to work on a certain strengthening of the ether body systematically in upbringing and in school, so that it occurs even in youth. Here what Anthroposophy suggests today will not be carried out for a long time, because the authorities in question will count Anthroposophy as something strange for a long time; but it doesn't matter. Let us assume that in teaching children to write, we first teach them a certain style of writing, and then, after a few years, we simply change the writing style without any other reason than to do so. Then the change in handwriting and the strengthening of the attention that would have to come about during the change would have an enormously strengthening influence on the developing ether body, and many of the nervous conditions people have would not come up.

So you see that one can do something in life that strengthens the ether body, and this is of extraordinary importance. It is precisely the weakness of the ether body that leads to the numerous really unhealthy situations in the present time. It can even be said—and truly, it is not saying too much—that certain forms of disease, which may very well be based in things about which nothing can be done, would run a very different course if the ether body were stronger than they run in the case of a weakened ether body, which is a standard feature of contemporary humanity. With this we have pointed to something that can be referred to as working on the ether body. We apply certain things to the ether body. One cannot apply anything at all to something that isn't there, something that can be denied. By showing that it is useful to do certain things with the etheric body, and by being able to prove that these things have an effect, one is showing that something like the etheric body does exist. Everywhere life offers the appropriate proofs of what Anthroposophy has to give us.

Our etheric body can also grow fundamentally stronger if we do something else to improve our memory. Perhaps in another connection this has already been mentioned here. However, for all forms of disease in which nervousness plays a part, one should certainly take advice drawn from this area as well. That is, one can do an enormous amount to strengthen the etheric body if one remembers the things one knows not only in the normal order one knows them but also remembering them backward. Let us say that in school someone has to learn a string of rulers or battles or other events. They are learned according to the year in which they occurred. It is extraordinarily good not only to have them learned or to learn them oneself in the normal order, but also to learn the matter in the reverse order, running through everything for oneself from back to front. This is an extraordinarily important matter. For if we do something like this in a more comprehensive way, we contribute once again to an enormous strengthening of our etheric body. To think through whole dramas backward to the beginning, or stories we have read, these are things that are important to the highest degree for the consolidation of the etheric body.

Now, you will be able to see that today people do not apply in life any of what we have just been discussing. In the contemporary restless racing of the day, we have very little chance to arrive at the inner peace that allows us to carry out such exercises. Normally a working person is too tired by evening to think any of the thoughts we have been discussing. But if Spiritual Science penetrates into people's hearts and souls, then they will realize that we could really do without an infinite amount of what goes on these days, and actually everyone can take the amount of time necessary for strengthening exercises of this kind. People would see very quickly, especially if they took pains with such things in the realm of education, that enormously favorable results are the consequences.

Let us mention another triviality, which to be sure is not so very useful in later life, but if a person has not cultivated it in early youth, then it is good to practice it in later life. That is to look again at certain things we accomplish, regardless of whether they leave a trace or not. This is relatively easy with regard to what we write. I am even convinced that many people could disabuse themselves of ugly handwriting if they tried, letter by letter, to look at what they have written, really to let their eyes pass again over what they have just written. This is possible to do quite well. Nevertheless, there is still another exercise that is very useful. That is, try to look at how we walk, how we move our hands, our head, how we laugh, and so forth—in short, if we try to give ourselves a pictorial account of our gestures. Very few people (this is something you can realize if you observe life closely enough) know how they walk. Very few have an idea of how it looks to someone who notices this. But it is good to do some of that, to gain a mental picture of oneself. For if we apply this sort of thing in life we will doubtlessly correct much of what we do (as indicated, it must not be pursued too far or it contributes too much toward human vanity), but, apart from that, it can have an enormously favorable effect on the consolidation of the etheric body, and also on the control of the etheric body by the astral body. And when we observe our gestures, when we look at what we do, when we have a mental image of our deeds, the control of the etheric body by the astral body grows ever stronger and stronger. That is, we arrive at the point where we can even, if necessary, suppress something we do. As things stand, people are less and less able to suppress something habitual at will, or to do something differently. But one of the greatest achievements of the human being is the ability to do what one does differently at times.

We are not trying to establish a handwriting school here; these days people might want to learn to alter their handwriting only to use it dishonestly. But as long as one undertakes to be perfectly honorable about it, it is good for the consolidation of the etheric body to take on a different handwriting. And in general it is good to acquire the ability to do things one has planned in a different way, not to be set on doing something only in one way. So we do not need to be fanatical advocates of equal facility with both hands, but if we nevertheless attempt in a moderate way to do certain tasks with the left hand (we need not force it beyond what we can really do), then this favorably influences the control that our astral body should exercise over our etheric body. Strengthening the human being in the way offered by spiritual scientific insight is something that should be brought to our culture through the spread of Spiritual Science.

And in fact this is something of great import—it could be called the cultivation of the will. Earlier we emphasized that nervousness expresses itself precisely in the confusion people often feel today about how to set about doing what they really wish to do or actually should wish to do. They draw back from carrying out what they have undertaken; they don't bring it off, and so on. This can be formulated as a certain weakness of the will, and it is caused by a lack of control of the astral body by the "I." There is always insufficient control of the astral body by the "I" when this kind of weakness of will appears; it is as if people simultaneously want something and don't want it, or at least don't manage to really carry out what they want. Many do not even manage to want earnestly what they want to want. Now, there is a simple means to strengthen the will for the outer life. The means is this: to suppress wishes that are doubtless there, not to act on them, if non-action on the wishes is not harmful and is possible. For if we examine ourselves in life, we find from morning to night countless things that we want, which it would be nice to have, but we also find many such wishes that we can forego, without harming someone else and without neglecting our own responsibilities: wishes whose satisfaction would give a certain pleasure, but which could also remain unsatisfied. If, then, one proceeds systematically, one can find among one's many wishes those of which it can be said, No, now I will not fulfill that wish. This is not to be done in the wrong way, but only with something that leads to no harm, whose fulfillment would bring nothing but comfort, happiness, pleasure. If we systematically suppress wishes of this kind, then every suppression of a kind of wish means an increase in strength of will, in the strength of the "I" over the astral body. If later in life we submit ourselves to such a procedure, then we will be able to make up, in this regard, for much that education currently neglects in many ways.

Now it is actually quite difficult to work effectively in this area, for one has to take into account that even if one, as a teacher, let's say, is in the position of being able to satisfy some emerging wish of a child or some young person, and refuses the wish, then not only a simple non-action may be set up, but also a kind of antipathy. But this can be harmful in a pedagogical sense, so that one could perhaps say: Yes, it looks doubtful whether one should introduce into one's educational principles the non-fulfillment of wishes of the students. One stands here before a real dilemma. If a father wants to educate his son by saying as often as possible, "No, Karl, you can't have that!," then he will more definitely evoke the boy's distaste for himself than he will achieve the good that is aimed at through non-fulfillment of wishes. The question arises: What is to be done? And one could simply not introduce such things at all.

But there is a very simple way to introduce it: One refuses the wishes, not to the young person, but to oneself, but in such a way that the young person is aware that one has foregone this or that. Now, in the first seven years of life, but even later as an aftereffect, a strong imitative drive is in effect, and we shall see, if we forego this or that in the presence of those we have to educate, that they imitate this, they see it as something worth striving for; and with this we will be doing something enormously significant.

So we see that our thoughts need only be led and directed in the right way through what Spiritual Science can be for us. Then Spiritual Science will not be theory; it will become life-wisdom, really something that supports us and carries us further in life.

An important means of strengthening the control of our "I" over the astral body can be learned to a certain extent from the two public lectures that I held here.* The special thing about these two lectures was that what could be said both for and against a thing was introduced. If you test how people position themselves in life in terms of their souls, you will see that generally when people have to act or think, they actually only say what can be said either for or against a thing. That is the norm. But there is nothing in life that cannot be handled in such a way that there is both a pro and a con—nothing at all. There is a pro and a con for everything, and it is good if we accustom ourselves always to take into account not only the one but also the other, not only the pro or the con, but also the pro and the con. Even for things that we then actually do, it is good to present to oneself why we would do better under certain circumstances not to do it or simply, if it is better to do it, to make clear to oneself that there are also reasons against doing it.

---

* Lecture in Munich, Jan. 8 and 10: *Wie widerlegt man Theosophie?* (How does one refute Theosophy?) and *Wie begrundet man Theosophy?* (How does one establish Theosophy?). These lectures were not fully transcribed and therefore are not included in the Collected Works (CW). Parallel lectures, however, were given in Berlin and are printed in *Ergebnisse der Geistesforschung* (Results of Spiritual Research; CW 62).

Vanity generally contradicts the notion that one should bring up the counter arguments against what one does, since people want only too much to be purely good. A person can seem to offer proof of being a good person by saying: I do only what there are good reasons for. And it is uncomfortable to realize that there are also many objections for almost everything that one does in life. We are really (I say it because it is extraordinarily important for life—not at all as good as we think. But this generalization has little purpose; it only has a purpose if in the individual things one does, despite carrying them out, since life does demand them, one also considers what could lead us to forego them. What this achieves can be presented to our soul in the following simple way: You will certainly have already encountered people who are weak-willed in the sense that they would rather not decide anything for themselves, but always prefer that the other person make the decision for them, so that they only have to carry out what they are supposed to do. They dump the responsibility, so to speak, and prefer to ask what they are supposed to do instead of finding the reasons for this or that action by themselves. Now, I do not introduce this case in order to present it as important in itself, but to achieve something else.

Let us take a person of this kind, who likes to ask others— mind you, what I have said is something that can be easily objected to, as well as assented to; one can hardly utter anything in life that couldn't be refuted in some fashion. Let us take such a person confronting two people who give advice on the same issue. One says, Yes!; the other says, Don't do it! Then we will experience in life that one adviser wins out over the other adviser. The one who has a stronger influence on that person's will wins out over the other. What kind of phenomenon is this really? As insignificant as it seems, it is a highly significant phenomenon.

If I stand before two people, one of whom says yes, the other no, and I carry out the yes, then that will works on in me, that strength of will has made itself felt in such a way that it empowered me to my action. One person's strength of will won out in me over the other person; the strength of that human being was victorious in me.

Now, assume that I am not standing before two other people, one of whom says yes and the other no, but that I stand there quite alone and bring out for myself the yes or no in my own heart, and bring up the reasons for each one; no one else comes to me, but I myself bring up the reasons for and against the matter. That develops a strong power, but now it is within myself. What earlier was exercised in me by the other person, I have now developed for myself as strength within my soul. Therefore, if I pose a choice to myself inwardly, I allow strength to conquer weakness. This is enormously important, because this again strengthens the control of the "I" over the astral body tremendously. Now we should not regard this as something unpleasant—to really honestly test the pros and cons in every individual case, wherever possible—and if we attempt to carry out what we have been describing, we will then see that a great deal has been achieved toward strengthening the will.

However, the issue also has a shadow side—that instead of strengthening the will, a weakening can emerge. This occurs if, after evaluating the pros and cons for oneself, one then does not act under the influence of one or the other power, but rather does nothing at all, out of negligence, following neither the one way nor the other. It seems then that one has obeyed the no, but really one has simply been lazy. Consequently, it is a good idea not to proceed with the self-presentation of pros and cons when you are tired, nor in any way worn out, but only when you feel strong, so that you know: I am not worn out, I can really follow through with the reason for presenting the pros and cons to myself. So care must be taken to allow these things to have an effect on the soul at the proper time.

Among the things that strengthen the control of our "I" over our astral body, it is important to divert from our souls everything that in any way sets up a contradiction between our environment and us. Of course, it is not among the duties of the anthroposophist to forbid oneself justified criticism. If the criticism is appropriate, then naturally it would be a weakness to pretend that what is bad is good—for purely spiritual scientific reasons, so to speak. However, we needn't do anything of the kind. Still, we have to learn to distinguish between what we criticize for its own sake and what we find uncomfortable, irritating, because of its influence on our own personality. The more we can accustom ourselves to make the judgment of our fellow humans independently of the way they stand in relation to ourselves, the better it is for the strengthening of our "I"-being in its control over the astral body. It is even good to impose on ourselves a certain renunciation, but not so as to be able to boast to ourselves that we are good people if we don't criticize our neighbors; rather, to make ourselves strong, we should strive not to be distressed by things that we might find distressing only because they are unpleasant to ourselves. Precisely in the area of judging our neighbors, the task would be to apply negative judgments preferably where one doesn't come into the picture oneself in any way. We will soon see that although this looks easy as a theoretical proposition, it is extraordinarily difficult to practice in real life. It is good, for example, when you have been lied to by someone to hold in check your antipathy that arises from having been lied to. It is not a question of going to others and further purveying the story that has been told, but simply of holding back the feeling of antipathy from that person having lied to you.

We can certainly use what we notice about people from one day to the next, the way their actions fit together, toward a judgment about them. If people talk one way at one time, and another way at another time, then we need only compare what they do, and we have a very different basis for judging them than if we emphasize their behavior to ourselves. And this is important— that we allow things as such to speak for themselves, or that we understand people as such from their own actions, not judging from individual behaviors but from how their actions fit together. We will find that even with regard to someone whom we consider thoroughly despicable, thinking: "This person never does anything that would not conform to this concept"—that even with such a person we find a great deal that does not fit in, that contradicts what he or she does. One need not take into account at all the relationship toward oneself; one can disregard it, and place people before one's soul in terms of their own conduct, if it is necessary to judge them at all. But it strengthens the "I" if we consider that we could well give up most, perhaps nine-tenths, of the judgments we make. If one experienced only a tenth of the judgments one makes about the world—really only a tenth—that would be richly sufficient for life. It would not compromise our lives in any way, not even for ourselves, if we decided to forego the remaining nine-tenths of the judgments that we so often make.

It may appear that I have presented trivialities today, but considering such things is our task from time to time. For it can be shown how trivialities can have great effects, and how we must get hold of life by quite other means than we normally do if we are to construct our life in a strong and healthy way. It is not always correct to say, "Well, if people are sick, let them go to the drugstore and there they will find what they need." It would be better for them to order their lives so that they are struck by illness less often, or that sicknesses become less oppressive. This will be possible if through such trivial things as I have just presented a person strengthens the influence of the "I" over the astral body, of the astral body over the etheric body, and of the etheric body over the physical body. Self-education as well as contribution to the education of others are things that can proceed from our fundamental anthroposophic conviction.

3

THE BOOK OF KNOWLEDGE

Excerpts from *Theosophy* by Rudolf Steiner

1. THE ESSENTIAL NATURE OF THE HUMAN BEING

We are bound up with the world in three different ways. The first way is something we encounter and accept as a given fact; through the second way, we turn the world into something that concerns us and has significance for us; the third way we hold as a goal to strive for unceasingly.

Why does the world appear to us in this threefold manner? A simple example can make it clear. Suppose I walk through a field where wildflowers are blooming. The flowers reveal their colors to me through my eyes—that is the fact I accept as given. When I then take pleasure in the wonderful display of colors, I am turning the fact into something that concerns me personally—that is, by means of my feelings, I relate the flowers to my own existence. A year later, when I go back to the same field, new flowers are there and they arouse new joy in me. The previous year's enjoyment rises up as a memory; it is present in me although the object that prompted it in the first place is gone. And yet the flowers I am now seeing are of the same species as last year's and have grown in accordance with the same laws. If I am familiar with this species and these laws, I will recognize them again in this year's flowers, just as I did in last year's. On reflection, I may realize that since last year's flowers are gone, my enjoyment of them remains only in my memory; it is bound up with my personal existence alone. But what I recognized in the flowers both last year and this year will remain as long as such flowers grow; it is something that is revealed to me but is not dependent on my existence in the same way that my enjoyment is. My feelings of pleasure remain within me, while the laws, the essence of the flowers, exist in the world outside of me.

31. How does the world appear in this threefold manner? Can you think of other examples (other than wildflowers) of relating to the world in this threefold way of fact, feeling, essence?

Thus, as human beings, we are constantly linking ourselves to the things of the world in a threefold way. (We should not read anything into this fact at first, but simply take it as it stands.) It shows us that there are three aspects to our human nature. For the moment, this and only this is what will be meant here by the three terms body, soul, and spirit. Associating any preconceived ideas or even hypotheses with these words will cause us to misunderstand the discussion that follows. By body is meant the means by which the things in our environment, such as the wildflowers in the example above, reveal themselves to us. The word soul designates the means by which we link these things to our own personal existence, by which we experience likes and dislikes, pleasure and displeasure, joy and sorrow. By spirit is meant what becomes apparent in us when, as "quasi-divine beings," to use Goethe's expression, we look at the things of the world. In this sense, each person consists of body, soul, and spirit.

Through the body, we are capable of linking ourselves for the moment to things outside us. Through the soul, we preserve the impressions things make on us. Through the spirit, what the things themselves contain is disclosed to us. Only when we look at the human being from these sides can we hope to understand our true nature, for these three sides show us that we are related to the rest of the world in a threefold way.

Through the body, we are related to the things that present themselves to our senses from outside. The substances of the outer world make up the body, and the forces of the outer world are active in it. We can observe our own bodily existence with our senses, just as we observe the things of the outside world, but it is not possible to observe our soul existence in the same way. With my bodily senses, I can observe the whole range of bodily processes taking place in me, but neither I nor anyone else can perceive my likes and dislikes or my joys and sorrows with bodily senses. The domain of the soul is inaccessible to bodily perception. Our bodily existence is there for all to see, but we carry our soul existence inside us as our own private world. Through the spirit, however, the outer world is revealed to us in a higher way. Although it is true that the secrets of the outer world disclose themselves inside us, in the spirit we step outside of ourselves and let the things themselves tell us what is significant for them, rather than for us. When we look up at the starry sky, the soul's experience of delight belongs to us, but the eternal laws of the stars, which we may grasp in thought and in spirit, do not belong to us. They belong to the stars.

Thus, as human beings we are citizens of three worlds. In body, we both belong to and perceive the outer world; in soul, we build up our own inner world; and in spirit, a third world that is higher than both of the others reveals itself to us.

32. Looking at the various professions available today, are there some that are more concerned with understanding the body, some more with the soul, and some with the spirit? If so, what are they? And are there some that are more inclined to look holistically at all three? Why?

The human body is built up in such a way that it meets the requirements of thinking; that is, the same substances and forces that are also present in the mineral kingdom are put together in the human body in a way that allows thinking to appear. For purposes of the following discussion, we will call this mineral structure, formed in accordance with its function, "the physical body" of the human being.

A body that is merely material—for example, a crystal—owes its form to the physical formative forces inherent in lifeless matter; a living body, however, cannot owe its form to these same forces, since it starts to decay immediately once life has abandoned it and it has been surrendered to physical forces alone. The life body is present at every moment of life as an entity that constantly maintains the physical body against decay.

Just as we belong to the mineral world through our physical body, we belong to the world of life through our ether body. After death, the physical body disintegrates into the mineral world, the ether body into the world of life. The term "body" is used here to designate what gives a being of any kind its form, shape, or Gestalt. It should not be confused with the sense-perceptible form of the material body. As used in this book, the term "body" can also refer to something that takes on form in soul or in spirit.

Picture human beings receiving impressions from all sides. Our sensations respond to all these impressions, so we also picture ourselves as the source of the sentient activity described above, which moves out in all the directions from which we receive impressions. We will call this source of activity the sentient soul.

With regard to perceiving the sentient soul, we must say something similar to what was said earlier about the ether body. Our bodily organs are blind to the sentient soul, and so is the organ by which life can be perceived as life, by which the ether body can be perceived. But by means of a still higher organ, the inner world of sensations can become a particular kind of suprasensory perception. As we develop this organ, we become able not only to sense the impressions of the physical and ether worlds, but also to see the sensations as such.

In its functioning, the sentient soul is dependent on the ether body, because it draws from the ether body what it then allows to light up as sensation. And since the ether body is the life within the physical body, the sentient soul is indirectly dependent on the physical body as well. Only a properly functioning and well-formed eye makes accurate color sensations possible. This is how the bodily nature affects the sentient soul. The sentient soul is thus determined and restricted in its activity by the physical body, and lives within the limits set by our bodily nature. That is, the physical body, which is built up out of mineral substances and enlivened by the ether body, in turn sets the limits for our sentient soul. Those who possess the above-mentioned organ for "seeing" the sentient soul therefore recognize it as having limits set by the body. However, the boundaries of the sentient soul do not coincide with those of the material physical body. The sentient soul extends beyond the physical body, even though the force that determines its limits proceeds from the physical body. This means that still another distinct member of the human constitution inserts itself between the physical and ether bodies on the one hand and the sentient soul on the other. This is the sentient or soul body. To say it another way, a portion of the ether body is finer than the rest, and this finer part forms a unity with the sentient soul, while the coarser part forms a kind of unity with the physical body. However, the sentient soul extends beyond the soul body.

For the sake of simplicity, we have chosen the term *sentient soul,* which is related to "sensing." But in fact, *sensing* is only one aspect of the soul's being. Our feelings of pleasure and displeasure, our drives, instincts, and passions, are all very close to our sensations. They are all similarly private and individual in character and similarly dependent on our bodily nature.

33. Name a film or book you encountered recently and describe how it appealed to the sentient soul of human nature.

Through thinking, we are led beyond our own personal lives; we acquire something that extends beyond our own souls. We seek the truth in our soul; through this truth, not only the soul but also the things of the world express themselves. Truth recognized through thinking has an independent significance, which refers to the things of the world and not merely to our own souls.

This applies equally to what is truly good. What is morally right is independent of our inclinations and passions insofar as it does not submit to them but makes them submit to it. Desire and revulsion, likes and dislikes, are the property of each individual human soul, but duty stands higher than likes and dislikes, sometimes standing so high in people's estimation that they will give up their lives for it. The more we have ennobled our inclinations, our likes and dislikes, so that they submit without force or compulsion to what we recognize as our duty, the higher we stand as human beings. What is morally right, like what is true, has an intrinsic eternal value that it does not receive from the sentient soul.

By letting what is intrinsically true and good come to life within us, we rise above the mere sentient soul. The eternal spirit shines into the sentient soul, kindling in it a light that will never go out. To the extent that our soul lives in this light, it takes part in something eternal, which it links to its own existence. What the soul carries within itself as truth and goodness is immortal. We will call this eternal element that lights up within the soul the consciousness soul.

The consciousness soul is different from the mind soul, which is still entangled in sensations, drives, emotions, and so forth. We all know how we accept our personal preferences as true, at first. But truth is lasting only when it has freed itself from any flavor of such sympathies and antipathies. The truth is true, even if all our personal feelings revolt against it. We will apply the term "consciousness soul" to that part of the soul in which truth lives.

34. Plato also spoke of "virtues" such as truth and goodness. The preceding passage states that what the soul carries within itself as truth and goodness is immortal. Why? How do you think this was meant?

Thus the soul, like the body, consists of three distinct members—the sentient soul, the mind soul, and the consciousness soul. Just as our bodily nature works from below upward to set limits on the soul, spirituality works from above downward to expand it. The more our soul is filled with what is true and good, the broader and more inclusive its eternal aspect becomes.

We all know that little children refer to themselves by saying things like "Charlie's a good boy" or "Mary wants that," and we find it appropriate that they should speak about themselves as they would about someone else, since they are not yet aware of their own independent existence. Consciousness of self has not yet been born in them.

Through this consciousness of self, an individual achieves self-definition as an independent being, separate from everything else, as "I." By "I," a person means the total experience of his or her being as body and soul. Body and soul are the vehicles of the "I";

it works in them. Just as the physical body has its center in the brain, the soul has its center in the "I." Our sensations are stimulated from outside; our feelings assert themselves as effects of the outer world; our will relates to the outer world by manifesting in outward-directed actions. Our "I," however, our actual individual essence, remains invisible.

This "I" is the self of each human being. We are justified in seeing the "I" as our true being, and may therefore describe body and soul as the "garments" in which we live, as the bodily conditions under which we act. In the course of our development we learn to use these instruments more and more as servants of our "I."

The "I" takes in the rays of the light that shines as eternal light in each human being. Just as we gather up experiences of body and soul in the "I," we also allow thoughts of truth and goodness to flow into it. Sense-perceptible phenomena reveal themselves to our "I" from one side, the spirit from the other. Body and soul give themselves over to the "I" in order to serve it, but the "I" gives itself over to the spirit in order to be filled by it. The "I" lives within the body and the soul, but the spirit lives within the "I." What there is of spirit in the "I" is eternal, for the "I" receives its nature and significance from whatever it is united with. To the extent that it dwells in a physical body, it is subject to mineral laws; through the ether body it is subject to the laws governing reproduction and growth; by virtue of the sentient and mind souls it is subject to the laws of the soul world. And to the extent that it receives the spiritual into itself, it is subject to the laws of the spirit. What is formed in accordance with mineral laws and the laws of life comes into existence and passes away again; the spirit, however, has nothing to do with becoming and perishing.

The "I" dwells in the soul. Although the highest manifestation of the "I" belongs to the consciousness soul, it is also true that the "I" radiates outward from there, filling the entire soul and exerting its influence on the body through the soul. And within the "I," the spirit is alive and active. The spirit streams into the "I," taking it as its "garment" just as the "I" itself lives in the body and the soul. The spirit shapes the "I" from the inside out and the mineral world shapes it from the outside in. We will call the spirit that shapes an "I," that lives as an "I," the spirit self, since it appears as the human "I" or "self."

35. Is there a part of your inner essence that no one else can see or even fully experience? Is it connected to your name, your picture of yourself? Have you ever thought of renaming yourself? Why or why not?

The physical body is built up within the physical world as a completely separate being, and the same is true of the spiritual body in the spiritual world. The human being likewise has an inside and an outside in the physical world, and the same is true in the spiritual world. And just as we take in substances from our physical surroundings and incorporate them into our bodies, we also take in spiritual substance from our spiritual surroundings and make it our own. This spiritual substance is eternal nourishment for human beings. We are born out of the physical world, and yet we are independent beings separate from the rest of the physical world. In the same way, we are born out of the spirit through the eternal laws of the good and the true, and yet we are separate from the spiritual world outside us. We will call this independent spiritual entity the "spirit body."

When we examine a physical human body, we find the same substances and forces that are found outside it in the rest of the physical world. The same is true of the spirit body—the elements of the outer spiritual world pulsate in it; the forces of the rest of the spiritual world are active in it. In the physical world, a living and sentient being is closed off within a physical skin, and the same applies to the spiritual world. A membrane closes off the spirit body from the undifferentiated spiritual world and makes the spirit body a self-contained spiritual being within that world, a being that intuitively perceives the spiritual content of the universe.

Just as we speak of an *ether body,* we must also speak of an *ether spirit* for the spirit body. We will call this ether spirit the *life spirit.* The spiritual constitution of the human being is thus subdivided into three members: the spirit body, the life spirit, and the spirit self.

If we want to comprehend the human being as a whole, we must imagine that each individual is put together out of the components described above. The physical body builds itself up out of the world of physical substance in such a way that this structure meets the requirements of a thinking "I." This body is permeated by life force, thus becoming the ether body or life body. As such, it opens itself up to the outside in the sense organs, and becomes the soul body. The soul body is permeated by, and forms a unity with, the sentient soul. The sentient soul not only receives the impressions of the outer world in the form of sensations but also has a life of its own that is fructified both by sensations from one side and by thinking from the other. Through this it can become the "mind soul." By being open to intuitions from above, just as it is open to sensations from below, it becomes the consciousness soul. This is possible because the spiritual world builds the organ of intuition into it, just as the physical body builds the sense organs for it. The senses transmit sensations to it by means of the soul body; similarly, the spirit transmits intuitions to it by means of the organ of intuition. Thus, the spirit body and the consciousness soul are linked in an entity analogous to the linking of the physical body and the sentient soul in the soul body. That is, the consciousness soul and the spirit self are a unity in which the spirit body lives as the life spirit, just as the ether body forms the living, bodily basis for the soul body. And just as the physical body is contained within the physical skin, the spirit body is also contained within the spiritual skin. As a result, the entire human being is subdivided into the following members:

1. Material, physical body
2. Ether body or life body
3. Soul body
4. Sentient soul
5. Mind soul
6. Consciousness soul
7. Spirit self
8. Life spirit
9. Spirit body

36. Some might say that the world today values and acknowledges the physical body and the intellect or mind soul above all else. If you agree, why do you think this is so? If not, why? Whether or not you agree with all the terms used in the above passages, do you think that there is more to a human being than a physical body and an intellect and if so, what?

2. DESTINY AND THE REINCARNATION OF THE SPIRIT

The soul stands between the present and the permanent in that it occupies the middle ground between body and spirit. However, it also mediates between the present and the permanent. It preserves the present for remembrance, wresting it away from perishability and giving it a place in the permanence of its own spiritual nature. The soul also puts the stamp of permanence on the temporal and temporary, since it does not simply give itself up to fleeting stimuli but also determines things out of its own initiative, incorporating its own essence into the actions it carries out. Through memory, the soul preserves yesterday; through action, it prepares tomorrow.

Whether or not I made an impression on someone else through something I have done depends on the presence or absence of something in the relationship of the world to my "I." I am a different person in my relationship to the world once I have made an impression on my environment. We do not notice this as easily as we notice how the "I" changes through acquiring a memory, but this is only because as soon as a memory is formed it unites with the overall life of the soul we have always regarded as our own, while the external consequence of an action, released from this soul life, goes on working through aftereffects that are quite different from what we can remember about the action. In spite of this, we must admit that something is now in the world as a result of our completed action, something whose character has been stamped on it by the "I."

Thinking this through carefully, we arrive at a question: Could it be that the results of our actions, whose character has been impressed on them by the "I," have a tendency to come back to the "I" in the same way that an impression preserved in memory comes to life again when an outer circumstance evokes it? What is preserved in memory is waiting for a reason to reappear. Could I be the same with things in the outer world that have been made lasting by the character of the "I"? Are they waiting to approach the soul from outside, just as a memory waits for a reason to approach from inside?

Remembering means experiencing something that is no longer there, linking a past experience to my present life. This happens in every instance of remembering. Suppose I meet someone I recognize because I met him or her yesterday. This person would be a total stranger to me if I could not link the image formed through yesterday's perception to my impression of today. Today's image is given to me by perception, that is, by my sensory system. But who conjures up yesterday's image into my soul? It is the same being in me who was present at both yesterday's encounter and today's. Throughout the preceding discussion, this being has been called "the soul." Without this trusty keeper of the past, every external impression would be a new one for us. The soul imprints on the body the process by which something becomes a memory. However, the soul must first do the imprinting, and then perceive its imprint just as it perceives something outside itself. In this way, the soul is the keeper of memory. As the keeper of the past, the soul is continually collecting treasures for the spirit. My ability to distinguish right from wrong is due to the fact that as a human being, I am a thinking being capable of grasping truth in my spirit. The truth is eternal; even if I were continually losing sight of the past and each impression were new to me, the truth could still always reveal itself to me again in things. But the spirit in me is not restricted to the impressions of the moment; my soul widens the spirit's field of vision to include the past. And the more my soul can add to the spirit from the past, the richer the spirit becomes. The soul passes on to the spirit what it has received from the body. Thus, at every moment of its life, the human spirit carries two very different elements—first, the eternal laws of the true and the good; second, the recollection of past experiences. Whatever it does is accomplished under the influence of these two factors. Therefore, if we want to understand a human spirit, we must know two different things about it—first, how much of the eternal has been revealed to it, and second, how many treasures from the past it holds.

This is how the spirit transforms its treasure trove of memories. It abandons to fate anything that can lead only to images of individual experiences, keeping only the power to heighten its own abilities. We can be sure that not a single experience goes to waste, since the soul preserves each one as a memory, and the spirit extracts from each one whatever it can use to enhance its abilities and enrich its life. The human spirit grows as these experiences are worked over and assimilated.

> 37. As stated, "As the keeper of the past, the soul is continually collecting treasures for the spirit. We can be sure that not a single experience goes to waste, since the soul preserves each one as a memory, and the spirit extracts from each one whatever it can use to enhance its abilities and enrich its life. The human spirit grows as these experiences are worked over and assimilated." Have you ever known someone you would consider "wise" (a grandparent, teacher, friend)? If so, what were the "treasures preserved for the spirit" that you experienced in that person?

We cannot maintain that the spiritual differences in people result only from differences in their environment, their upbringing, and so on. That is not true at all, because two people from similar environments and of similar educational backgrounds can still develop in very different ways. We are forced to admit that they must have begun life with very different endowments.

The physical similarity between human beings is apparent to the eye, and the difference between human spiritual forms is equally apparent to the unbiased spiritual view. This is demonstrated by one very evident fact—that human beings have biographies. If we were nothing more than members of our species, no individual biographies would be possible. A lion or a pigeon is of interest only as a member of the lion or pigeon species; we understand everything essential about the individual once we have described the species. It does not really matter whether we are dealing with a parent, child, or grandchild—what is interesting about them is common to all three generations. What a human individual signifies, however, only begins where he or she stops being merely a member of a genus and species and becomes an individual being. I certainly cannot grasp the essential nature of Mr. John Doe by describing his son or his father—I have to know his own personal biography. If we think about the nature of biography, we will realize that with regard to the spirit, each human being is his or her individual genus.

As a physical human being, I am descended from other physical human beings; I have the same form or Gestalt as the rest of the human genus. This shows that the characteristics of a genus are acquired within it through heredity. But as a spiritual human being, I have my own particular form, just as I have a personal biography.

Therefore, I cannot have acquired this form from anyone other than myself. And since I came into this world, not with general, but with very specific predispositions of soul that have determined the course of my life as revealed by my biography, my work on myself cannot have begun at birth. I must have been present as a spiritual individual before my birth. I was certainly not present in my ancestors, because as spiritual individuals they are different from me, and their biographies cannot explain mine. Instead, I must—as a spiritual being—be the repetition of one whose biography can explain mine.

Schiller carried a physical form that he inherited from his ancestors; this physical form could not possibly have grown up out of the earth. The same is true of Schiller as a spiritual individuality; he must have been the repetition of another spiritual being whose biography accounts for his, just as human reproduction accounts for his physical form. The human physical form is a repetition or re-embodiment, over and over again, of what is inherent in the human genus and species. Similarly, a spiritual individual must be a re-embodiment or reincarnation of one and the same spiritual being, for as a spiritual being, each person is his or her own species.

> 38. Looking at your life story thus far, are there aspects of your biography that cannot be explained by hereditary influences? Please try and name at least one quality of yourself or a unique experience that must be "you" and not your family.

Human physical bodies differ only slightly on the basis of race, nation, and family, and although individual ether bodies vary more, they still show a great similarity.

However, when it comes to the soul body, the differences are already very great. In the soul body, what we perceive as a person's external personal uniqueness is expressed; the soul body is therefore also the carrier of whatever personal uniqueness is passed down from ancestors to descendants.

From the spirit, the soul receives the gift of living in the true and the good, and this enables it to bring the spirit itself to expression in its own life, in its inclinations, drives, and passions. The spirit self brings the eternal laws of the true and the good to the "I" from the world of the spirit. By means of our consciousness soul, these laws are linked to the soul's own individual life experiences. These experiences are transitory, but their fruits are lasting; the fact that they have been linked to the spirit self makes a lasting impression on it. If the human spirit then approaches such an experience and finds it similar to another that it has already been linked to in the past, it recognizes something familiar in it and knows that it must behave differently toward this than if it were encountering it for the first time. This is the basis of all learning. The fruits of learning are the abilities we acquire, and in this way, the fruits of our transitory life are imprinted on our immortal spirit.

Are we aware of these fruits in some way? Where do those potentials described above as characteristic of the spiritual human being come from? Surely they can only be based on the various capabilities people bring with them when they set out on their earthly journey. In some respects, these capabilities are quite like the ones we can acquire during our lifetime. Take the case of a genius, for instance. As a boy Mozart could write down from memory a long piece of music he had heard only once. He was able to do so only because he could survey the whole thing all at once, as a totality.

In each life the human spirit appears as a repetition of itself, with the fruits of its experiences in earlier lifetimes. Thus, this lifetime is the repetition of others, and brings with it what the spirit self has gained in its previous life. When the spirit self takes in something that can develop into fruit, it imbues itself with the life spirit. Just as the life body reproduces the form of a species from generation to generation, the life spirit reproduces the soul from one personal existence to the next.

39. How do you feel about the idea of reincarnation of the human spirit—the part of you that is purely you?

What someone did yesterday is still present today in the form of its effects.

Along these lines, the metaphor of sleep and death gives us a picture of the connection between cause and effect. Sleep has often been called "the younger brother of death." I get up in the morning. The continuity of my activity has been interrupted by the night. Under normal circumstances, I cannot resume my activity arbitrarily—I must link up with what I did yesterday if my life is to have any order and cohesiveness. Yesterday's actions are now the conditions I must abide by in what I do today; through what I did yesterday, I have created my destiny for today. I have disengaged myself from my own activity for a while, but it belongs to me and pulls me back again after I have withdrawn from it for a while. My past continues to be connected to me; it lives on in my present and will follow me into my future. Instead of waking up this morning, I would have to be created anew, out of nothing, if the effects of my actions from yesterday were not meant to be my destiny today. It would be as absurd as if under ordinary circumstances I had had a house built for myself and then did not move into it.

But we are not created anew each morning, nor is the human spirit created anew as it starts the journey of its earthly life. We must try to understand what really does happen when we set out on this journey. A physical body makes its appearance, having received its form through the laws of heredity. This body becomes the vehicle for a spirit that is repeating an earlier life in a new form. Between the two, leading a self-contained life of its own, stands the soul. It is served by its likes and dislikes, and its wishes and desires, and places thinking in its service. As the sentient soul, it receives impressions from the outer world and carries them to the spirit, which extracts and preserves their fruits. The soul plays a mediator's role, in a sense, and its task is accomplished in playing this role satisfactorily. The body forms impressions for the soul, which reshapes them into sensations, stores them in the memory as mental images, and passes them on to the spirit to be made lasting. The soul is what actually makes us belong to this earthly life. Through the body, we belong to the physical human genus; we are members of this genus. With our spirit, we live in a higher world. The soul binds the two worlds together for a while.

What we experience as destiny in one lifetime is related to our actions in previous earthly lives.

Through its actions, each human spirit has truly prepared its own destiny. It finds itself linked in each new lifetime to what it did in the previous one.

40. What are your thoughts and feelings about the last two sentences?

From the above, we can form an idea of how the soul is incorporated into the overall organization of a human being. The physical body is subject to the laws of heredity. The human spirit, on the other hand, must reincarnate over and over again, and its law consists in having to carry the fruits of previous lifetimes over into the following ones. Our souls live in the present, although this life in the present is not independent of our previous lives, since each incarnating spirit brings its destiny along with it from previous incarnations, and this destiny determines its present life. What impressions our souls will be capable of receiving, which of our desires can be fulfilled, what joys and sorrows will be our lot, what other human beings we will meet—all this depends on what our actions were like in earlier incarnations of the spirit.

People to whom our souls were connected in one lifetime will necessarily encounter us again in a later one, because the actions that took place between us must have their consequences. Souls that have once been associated will venture into reincarnation at the same time. Thus, the life of the soul is a product of the spirit's self-created destiny.

The body is subject to the laws of heredity; the soul is subject to self-created destiny or, to use an ancient term, to its karma; and the spirit is subject to the laws of reincarnation or repeated earthly lives. The interrelationship of body, soul, and spirit can also be expressed as follows: The spirit is immortal; birth and death govern our bodily existence in accordance with the laws of the physical world; and the life of the soul, which is subject to destiny, mediates between body and spirit during the course of an earthly life.

5

THE FOUR TEMPERAMENTS

Lecture in Berlin, March 4, 1909

It has been emphasized frequently that humanity's greatest mystery is itself. Both natural and spiritual science ultimately try to solve this riddle—natural science by understanding the natural laws that govern our outer being, science of the spirit by seeking the essence and inherent purpose of our existence. Now as correct as it may be that humanity's greatest riddle is itself, it must also be emphasized that each individual human being is a riddle, often even to itself. Every one of us experiences this in encounters with other people.

Today we shall be dealing not with general riddles, but rather with those posed to us by every human being in every encounter, and these are just as important. For how endlessly varied people are! We need only consider temperament, the subject of today's lecture, in order to realize that there are as many riddles as there are people. Even within the basic types known as the temperaments, such variety exists among people that the very mystery of existence seems to express itself within these types. Temperament, that fundamental coloring of the human personality, plays a role in all manifestations of individuality that are of concern to practical life. We sense something of this basic mood whenever we encounter another human being. Thus, we can only hope that Spiritual Science will tell us what we need to know about the temperaments.

Our first impression of the temperaments is that they are external, for although they can be said to flow from within, they manifest themselves in everything we can observe from without. However, this does not mean that the human mystery can be solved by means of natural science and observation. Only when we hear what Spiritual Science has to say can we come closer to understanding these peculiar colorations of the human personality.

Spiritual Science tells us first of all that the human being is part of a line of heredity. A person displays the characteristics that were inherited from father, mother, grandparents, and so on. These characteristics are then passed on to the following progeny. The human being thus possesses certain traits by virtue of being part of a succession of generations.

However, this inheritance gives us only one side of human nature. Joined to that is the individuality that is brought out of the spiritual world. This is added to what father, mother, and other ancestors are able to give. Something that proceeds from life to life, from existence to existence, connects itself with the generational stream. Certain characteristics can be attributed to heredity; on the other hand, as a person develops from childhood on, we can see unfolding out of the center of this being something that must be the fruit of preceding lives, something that could never have been only inherited from ancestors. We come to know the law of reincarnation, of the succession of earthly lives, and this is but a special case of an all-encompassing cosmic law.

An illustration will make this seem less paradoxical. Consider a lifeless mineral—say, a rock crystal. Should the crystal be destroyed, it leaves nothing of its form that could be passed on to other crystals. A new crystal receives nothing of the old one's particular form.* When we move on to the world of plants, we notice that a plant cannot develop according to the same laws as the crystal. It can only originate from another, earlier plant. Form is here preserved and passed on.

Moving on to the animal kingdom, we find an ongoing evolution of the species. We begin to appreciate why the nineteenth century held the discovery of evolution to be its greatest achievement. In animals, not only does one being proceed from another, but each young animal during the embryo phase recapitulates the earlier phases of its species' evolutionary development. The species itself undergoes an enhancement.

Not only does the species evolve in human beings, but the individual also evolves. What a human being acquires in a lifetime through education and experience is preserved, just as surely as are the evolutionary achievements of an animal ancestral line. It will someday be commonplace to trace a person's inner core to a previous existence. The human being will come to be known as the product of an earlier life. The views that stand in the way of this doctrine will be overcome, just as was the scholarly opinion of an earlier century, which held that living organisms could arise from nonliving substances. As recently as three hundred years ago, scholars believed that animals could evolve from river

---

*   Translator's note: The reader may conclude from this remark (it was, after all, a remark, not a published claim) that Steiner was ignorant of the concept of seed crystals. However, a likelier explanation is that Steiner, whose audience was very likely not a scientifically knowledgeable one, was simply indulging in a bit of rhetorical hyperbole. He doubtless knew that a seed crystal will hasten the crystallization process in a saturated salt solution, but this fact is not really relevant to his point, which comes out only gradually in this paragraph. His point is not that a newly forming crystal cannot receive some contribution from a previously existing one, only that it need not; this is in contrast to living things, which require a progenitor.

mud, that is, from nonliving matter. Francesco Redi, an Italian scientist, was the first to assert that living things could develop only from other living things.[*] He was attacked for this and came close to suffering the fate of Giordano Bruno.[**] Today, burning people at the stake is no longer fashionable. When someone attempts to teach a new truth, for example, that psycho-spiritual entities must be traced back to earlier psycho-spiritual entities, that person won't exactly be burned at the stake, but will probably be dismissed as a fool. But the time will come when the real foolishness will be to believe that the human being lives only once, that there is no enduring entity that unites itself with a person's inherited traits.

Now the important question arises: How can something originating in a completely different world, that must seek a father and a mother, unite itself with physical corporeality? How can it clothe itself in the bodily features that link human beings to a hereditary chain? How does the spiritual-psychic stream, of which a human being forms a part through reincarnation, unite itself with the physical stream of heredity? The answer is that a synthesis must be achieved. When the two streams combine, each imparts something of its own quality to the other. In much the same way that blue and yellow combine to give green, the two streams in the human being combine to yield what is commonly known as temperament. Our inner self and our inherited traits both appear in it. Temperament stands between the things that connect a human being to an ancestral line, and those the human being brings out of earlier incarnations. Temperament strikes a

---

[*] Francesco Redi (1626–1697) refuted spontaneous generation of living beings from mud.

[**] Giordano Bruno (1548–1600) was an Italian philosopher and Dominican monk who was burned at the stake as a heretic. He taught that the world is infinite in space and time and filled with innumerable suns.

balance between the eternal and the ephemeral. It does so in such a way that the essential members of the human being, which we have come to know in other contexts, enter into a very specific relationship with one another.

Human beings as we know them in this life are beings of four members. The first, the physical body, they have in common with the mineral world. The first suprasensory member, the etheric body, is integrated into the physical and separates from it only at death. There follows as the third member the astral body, the bearer of instincts, drives, passions, desires, and of the everchanging content of sensation and thought. Our highest member places us above all other earthly beings as the bearer of the human "I," which endows us in such a curious and yet undeniable fashion with the power of self-awareness. These four members we have come to know as the essential constituents of a human being.

The way the four members combine is determined by the flowing together of the two streams upon a person's entry into the physical world. In every case, one of the four members achieves predominance over the others, and gives them its own peculiar stamp. Where the bearer of the "I" predominates, a choleric temperament results. Where the astral body predominates, we find a sanguine temperament. Where the etheric or life body predominates, we speak of a phlegmatic temperament. And where the physical body predominates, we have to deal with a melancholic temperament. The specific way in which the eternal and the ephemeral combine determines what relationship the four members will enter into with one another.

The way the four members find their expression in the physical body has also frequently been mentioned. The "I" expresses itself in the circulation of the blood. For this reason, in the choleric the predominant system is that of the blood. The astral body expresses itself physically in the nervous system; thus, in the sanguine, the nervous system holds sway. The etheric body expresses itself in the glandular system; hence the phlegmatic is dominated physically by the glands. The physical body as such expresses itself only in itself; the outwardly most important feature in the melancholic is therefore the physical body. This can be observed in all phenomena connected with these temperaments.

In the choleric, the "I" and the blood system predominate. Cholerics come across as people who must always have their own way. Their aggressiveness, everything connected with their forcefulness of will, derives from their blood circulation.

In the nervous system and astral body, sensations and feelings constantly fluctuate. Any harmony or order results solely from the restraining influence of the "I." People who do not exercise that influence appear to have no control over their thoughts and sensations. They are totally absorbed by the sensations, pictures, and ideas that ebb and flow within them. Something like this occurs whenever the astral body predominates, as, for example, in the sanguine. Sanguines surrender themselves in a certain sense to the constant and varied flow of images, sensations, and ideas, since in them the astral body and nervous system predominate.

The nervous system's activity is restrained only by the circulation of the blood. That this is so becomes clear when we consider what happens when a person lacks blood or is anemic—in other words, when the blood's restraining influence is absent. Mental images fluctuate wildly, often leading to illusions and hallucinations.

A touch of this is present in sanguines, who are incapable of lingering over an impression. They cannot fix their attention on a particular image nor sustain their interest in an impression. Instead, they rush from experience to experience, from percept to percept. This is especially noticeable in sanguine children, where it can be a source of concern. The sanguine child's interest is easily kindled, a picture will easily impress, but the impression quickly vanishes.

We proceed now to the phlegmatic temperament. We observed that this temperament develops when the etheric or life body, as we call it, which regulates growth and metabolism, is predominant. The result is a sense of inner well-being. The more human beings live in their etheric body, the more they are preoccupied with their own internal processes. They let external events run their course while their attention is directed inward.

In melancholics we have seen that the physical body, the coarsest member of the human organization, becomes master over the others. As a result, melancholics feel they are not master over their body, that they cannot bend it to their will. The physical body, which is intended to be an instrument of the higher members, is itself in control, and frustrates the others. Melancholics experience this as pain, as a feeling of despondency. Pain continually wells up within them because the physical body resists the etheric body's inner sense of well-being, the astral body's liveliness, and the purposeful striving of the "I."

The varying combinations of the four members also manifest themselves quite clearly in external appearance. People in whom the "I" predominates seek to triumph over all obstacles, to make their presence known. Accordingly, their "I" stunts the growth of the other members; it withholds from the astral and etheric bodies their due portion. This reveals itself outwardly in a very clear fashion. Johann Gottlieb Fichte, that famous German choleric, was recognizable as such purely externally.* His build revealed clearly that the lower essential members had been held back in

---

* Johann Gottlieb Fichte (1762–1814), German Idealist philosopher.

their growth. Napoleon, another classic example of the choleric, was so short because his "I" had held the other members back.* Of course, one cannot generalize that all cholerics are short and all sanguines tall. It is a question of proportion. What matters is the relation of size to overall form.

In the sanguine the nervous system and the astral body predominate. The astral body's inner liveliness animates the other members and makes the external form as mobile as possible. Whereas the choleric has sharply chiseled facial features, the sanguine's are mobile, expressive, changeable. We see the astral body's inner liveliness manifested in every outer detail, for example, in a slender form, a delicate bone structure, or lean muscles. The same thing can be observed in details of behavior. Even a nonclairvoyant can tell from behind whether someone is a choleric or a sanguine; one does not need to be a spiritual scientist for that. If you observe the gait of a choleric, you will notice that a choleric plants each foot so solidly that it would seem to bore down into the ground. By contrast, the sanguine has a light, springy step. Even subtler external traits can be found. The inwardness of the "I," the choleric's self-contained inwardness, expresses itself in eyes that are dark and smoldering. The sanguine, whose "I" has not taken such deep root, who is filled with the liveliness of his astral body, tends by contrast to have blue eyes. Many more such distinctive traits of these temperaments could be cited.

The phlegmatic temperament manifests itself in a static, indifferent physiognomy, as well as in plumpness, for fat is due largely to the activity of the etheric body. In all this the phlegmatic's inner sense of comfort is expressed. The gait is loose-jointed and shambling, and the manner timid. Phlegmatics seem somehow to be not entirely in touch with their surroundings.

---

* Napoleon Bonaparte (1769–1821) was a French ruler and emperor from 1804 to 1815.

The melancholic is distinguished by a hanging head, as if the strength necessary to straighten the neck was lacking. The eyes are dull, not shining as the choleric's are; the gait is firm, but in a leaden rather than a resolute sort of way.

You see, therefore, how significantly Spiritual Science can contribute to the solution of this mystery. Unless we seek to encompass reality in its entirety—which includes the spiritual—knowledge cannot bear practical fruit. Accordingly, only Spiritual Science can give us knowledge that will benefit the individual and all humankind. In education, very close attention must be paid to the individual temperaments, for it is especially important to be able to guide and direct them as they develop in the child. But the temperaments are also important to our efforts to improve ourselves later in life. We do well to attend to what expresses itself through them if we wish to further our personal development.

The four fundamental types I have outlined here for you naturally never manifest themselves in such pure form. Every human being has one basic temperament, with varying degrees of the other three mixed in. Napoleon, for example, although a choleric, had much of the phlegmatic in him. To master life truly, it is important that we open our souls to what manifests itself as typical. When we consider that the temperaments, each of which represents a mild imbalance, can degenerate into unhealthy extremes, we realize just how important this is.

Yet, without the temperaments the world would be an exceedingly dull place, not only ethically, but also in a higher sense. The temperaments alone make all multiplicity, beauty, and fullness of life possible. Thus, in education it would be senseless to want to homogenize or eliminate them, but an effort should be made to direct each into the proper track, for in every temperament there lie two dangers of aberration, one great, one small. One danger for young cholerics is that they will never learn to control their temper as they develop into maturity. That is the small danger. The greater is that they will become foolishly single-minded. For the sanguine the lesser danger is flightiness; the greater is mania, induced by a constant stream of sensations. The small danger for the phlegmatic is apathy; the greater is stupidity, dullness. For the melancholic, insensitivity to anything other than personal pain is the small danger; the greater is insanity.

In light of all this it is clear that to guide the temperaments is one of life's significant tasks. If this task is to be properly carried out, however, one basic principle must be observed, which is always to reckon with what is given, and not with what is not there. For example, if a child has a sanguine temperament, it will not be helped by elders who try to flog interest into the child. The temperament simply will not allow it. Instead of asking what the child lacks, in order that we might beat it in, we must focus on what the child has, and base ourselves on that. And as a rule, there is one thing that will always stimulate the sanguine child's interest. However flighty the child might be, we can always stimulate interest in a particular personality. If we ourselves are that personality, or if we bring the child together with someone who is, the child cannot but develop an interest. Only through the medium of love for a personality can the interest of the sanguine child be awakened. More than children of any other temperament, the sanguine needs someone to admire. Admiration is here a kind of magic word, and we must do everything we can to awaken it.

We must reckon with what we have. We should see to it that the sanguine child is exposed to a variety of things in which a deeper interest is shown. These things should be allowed to speak to the child, to have an effect upon the child. They should then be withdrawn, so that the child's interest in them will intensify; then they may be restored. In other words, we must fashion the sanguine's environment so that it is in keeping with the temperament.

The choleric child is also susceptible of being led in a special way. The key to this child's education is respect and esteem for a natural authority. Instead of winning affection by means of personal qualities, as we try to do with the sanguine child, we should see to it that the child's belief in the teacher's ability remains unshaken. The teacher must demonstrate an understanding of what goes on around the child. Any showing of incompetence should be avoided. The child must persist in the belief that the teacher is competent, or all authority will be lost. The magic potion for the choleric child is respect and esteem for a person's worth, just as for the sanguine child it is love for a personality. Outwardly, the choleric child must be confronted with challenging situations. The choleric must encounter resistance and difficulty, lest life become too easy.

The melancholic child is not easy to lead. With a melancholic, however, a different approach may be applied. For the sanguine child the approach is love for a personality; for the choleric, it is respect and esteem for a teacher's worth. By contrast, the important thing for the melancholic is that the teachers be people who have in a certain sense been tried by life, who act and speak on the basis of past trials. The child must feel that the teacher has known real pain. Let your treatment of life's details be an occasion for the child to appreciate what you have suffered. Sympathy with the destinies of others furthers the melancholic's development. Here, too, one must reckon with what the child has. The melancholic has a firmly rooted capacity for suffering, for discomfort, that cannot be disciplined out. However, it can be redirected. We should expose the child to legitimate external pain and suffering, so that the child learns there are outer things that can engage the capacity for experiencing pain. This is the essential thing. We should not try to divert or amuse the melancholic, for to do so only intensifies the despondency and inner suffering; instead, the melancholic child must be enabled to see that objective occasions for suffering exist in life. Although we must not carry it too far, redirecting the child's suffering to outside objects is what is called for.

The phlegmatic child should not be allowed to grow up alone. Although naturally all children should have playmates, for phlegmatics it is especially important that they have them. Their playmates should have the most varied interests. Phlegmatic children learn by sharing in the interests, the more numerous the better, of others. Their playmates' enthusiasms will overcome their native indifference toward the world. Whereas the important thing for the melancholic is to experience another person's destiny, for the phlegmatic child it is to experience the whole range of a playmate's interests. Phlegmatics are not moved by things as such, but interest arises when they see things reflected in others. Those interests are then reflected in the souls of phlegmatic children. We should bring to their environment objects and events toward which "phlegm" is an appropriate reaction. Impassivity must be directed toward the right objects—those toward which one may be phlegmatic.

From the examples of these pedagogical principles, we see how Spiritual Science can address practical problems. These principles can also be applied to oneself, for purposes of self-improvement. For example, a sanguine gains little by self-reproach. Our minds are in such questions frequently an obstacle. When pitted directly against stranger forces such as the temperaments, they can accomplish little. Indirectly, however, they can accomplish much. Sanguines, for example, can take their sanguinity into account, abandoning self-exhortation as fruitless. The important thing is to display sanguinity under the right circumstances. Experiences suited to a short attention span can be brought about through thoughtful planning. Using thought in this way, even on the smallest scale, will produce the requisite effect.

Those of a choleric temperament should purposely put themselves in situations where rage is of no use, but rather only makes them look ridiculous. Melancholics should not close their eyes to life's pain, but rather seek it out; through compassion they redirect their suffering outward toward appropriate objects and events. If we are phlegmatic, having no particular interests, then we should occupy ourselves as much as possible with uninteresting things, surround ourselves with numerous sources of tedium, so that we become thoroughly bored. We will then be thoroughly cured of our "phlegm"; we will have gotten it out of our system. Thus does one reckon with what one has, and not with what one does not have.

By filling ourselves with practical wisdom such as this, we learn to solve that basic riddle of life, the other person. It is solved not by postulating abstract ideas and concepts, but by means of pictures. Instead of arbitrarily theorizing, we should seek an immediate understanding of every individual human being. We can do this, however, only by knowing what lies in the depths of the soul. Slowly and gradually, Spiritual Science illuminates our minds, making us receptive not only to the big picture, but also to subtle details. Spiritual Science makes it possible that when two souls meet and one demands love, the other offers it. If something else is demanded, that other thing is given. We create the basis for society through such true, living wisdom.

This is what we mean when we say we must solve a mystery every moment.

Anthroposophy acts not by means of sermons, exhortations, or catechisms, but by creating a social groundwork upon which human beings can come to know each other. Spiritual Science is the ground of life, and love is the blossom and fruit of a life enhanced by it. Spiritual Science may thus claim to lay the foundation for a person's most beautiful goal—true, genuine love for humankind.

6

THE BOOK OF FREEDOM

Excerpts from *Intuitive Thinking as a Spiritual Path*
by Rudolf Steiner

LEAD QUESTIONS

41. Can we understand human nature in such a way that this understanding serves as the basis for everything else we may meet in the way of experience or science?

42. Can we, as human beings and volitional entities, ascribe freedom to ourselves, or is such freedom a mere illusion that arises because we do not see the threads of necessity upon which our willing, like any other natural event, depends?

43. As you read the following sections, consider the basic question that has confronted humankind since the beginning: Are we essentially free, or are we governed mostly by necessity? Are we a product of "nature or nurture"? Are we able to direct our lives through individual initiative or are we constrained mostly by surrounding circumstances?

1. CONSCIOUS HUMAN ACTION

I s a human being spiritually *free* or subject to the iron necessity of purely natural law?

Today, everyone who can claim to have outgrown scientific kindergarten appears to know that freedom cannot consist in choosing arbitrarily between two possible actions. There is always, so it is claimed, a quite specific *reason* why a person performs one specific action from among several possibilities.

Children, therefore, believe that they freely desire milk; an angry boy believes that he freely demands revenge; and coward believe that they freely choose to flee. Drunkards believe it is a free decision to say, once sober, what they wish that they had not said. Because this bias is inherent in all humans, it is not easy to free oneself from it.

Just as a stone necessarily carries out a specific movement in response to an impact, human beings are supposed to carry out an action by a similar necessity if impelled to it by any reason. Human beings imagine themselves to be the free originators of their actions only because they are aware of these actions. In so doing, however, they overlook the causes driving them, which they must obey unerringly. The error in this train of thought is easy to find. Spinoza and all who think like him overlook the human capacity to be aware not only of one's actions, but also of the causes by which one's actions are guided.

No one will dispute that a child is *unfree* when it desires milk, as is a drunkard who says things and later regrets them. Both know nothing of the causes, active in the depths of their organism, that exercise irresistible control over them. But is it justifiable to lump together actions of this kind with those in which humans are conscious not only of their actions but also of the reasons that motivate them? Are the actions of human beings really all of a single kind? Should the acts of a warrior on the battlefield, a scientist in the laboratory, a diplomat involved in complex negotiations, be set scientifically on the same level as that of a child when it desires milk?

And there is, after all, a profound difference between knowing and not knowing why I do something.

Can the question of the freedom of our will be posed narrowly by itself? And, if not, with what other questions must it necessarily be linked?

If there is a difference between a conscious motive and an unconscious drive, then the conscious motive will bring with it an action that must be judged differently from an action done out of blind impulse. Our first question will concern this difference. The position we must take on freedom itself will depend on the result of this inquiry.

44. How does our justice system take this into account? For example, premeditated acts of violence vs. self-defense. Describe the difference.

If a motive acts upon me, and I am forced to follow it because it proves to be the "strongest" of its kind, then the thought of freedom ceases to have any meaning. Why should it matter to me whether I can do something or not, if I am *forced* by the motive to do it? The first question is not whether I can or cannot do something once the motive has operated upon me, but whether there exist only motives of the kind that operate with compelling necessity. If *I have to* will something, then I may even be utterly indifferent as to whether I can actually do it. If, because of my character and the circumstances prevailing in my environment, a motive were forced upon me that my thinking showed me was unreasonable, then I would even have to be glad if I could not do what I will.

It is not a question of whether I can execute a decision once it is made, but of *how the decision arises within me.*

There lies, between us and the action, the motive *that has become conscious.*

45. How can we become more conscious of our motives?

This leads us to ask: what is the origin and the significance of thinking? For without understanding the soul's activity of *thinking*, no concept of the knowledge of anything, including an action, is possible. When we understand what thinking means in general, it will be easy to clarify the role that thinking plays in human action. As Hegel rightly says, "Thinking turns the soul, with which beasts too are gifted, into spirit." Therefore, thinking will also give to human action its characteristic stamp.

As soon as our actions lift themselves above the satisfaction of purely animal desires, our motives are always permeated by thoughts. Love, pity, patriotism are springs of action that cannot be reduced to cold rational concepts. People say that the heart, the sensibility, comes into its own in such matters. No doubt. But heart and sensibility do not create the motives of action. They presuppose them and then receive them into their own realm. Pity appears in my heart when *the mental image* of a person who arouses pity in me enters my consciousness. The way to the heart goes through the head.

Love is no exception here. If it is not a mere expression of the sexual drive, then love is based on mental pictures that we form of the beloved. And the more idealistic these mental pictures are, the more blessed is the love. Here, too, thought is the father of feeling. People say that love makes us blind to the beloved's flaws. But we can also turn this around and claim that love opens our eyes to the beloved's strengths. Many pass by these good qualities without noticing them. One person sees them and, just for this reason, love awakens in the soul. What else has this person done but make a mental picture of what a hundred others have ignored? Love is not theirs because they lack the *mental picture.*

46. *Can you remember an instance in which love opened your eyes to another person?*

Or, can you recall an instance when your mental picture of a person led you to love that person, even when you were not at first inclined to do so? If so, what was it like?

2. THE FUNDAMENTAL URGE FOR KNOWLEDGE

Two souls, alas, dwell within my breast, each wants to separate from the other; one, in hearty love lust, clings to earth
with clutching organs; the other lifts itself mightily from the
dust to high ancestral regions. (Goethe, *Faust,* I, 1112)

With these words, Goethe characterizes a trait deeply
based in human nature. As human beings, we are not
organized in a fully integrated, unified way. We always demand
more than the world freely offers. Nature gives us needs, and
the satisfaction of some of these she leaves to our own activity.
The gifts allotted to us are abundant, but even more abundant
is our desire. We seem born for dissatisfaction. The urge to
know is only a special case of this dissatisfaction. We look at
a tree twice. The first time, we see its branches at rest, the
second time in motion. We are unsatisfied with this observation. Why, we ask, does the tree present itself to us now at
rest, now in motion? Every glance at nature engenders a host
of questions within us. We receive a new problem with each
phenomenon that greets us. Every experience becomes a riddle.
We see a creature similar to the mother animal emerging from
the egg, and we ask the reason for this similarity. We observe
a living creature's growth and development to a certain degree
of perfection, and we seek the conditions of this experience.
Nowhere are we content with what nature displays before our
senses. We look everywhere for what we call an *explanation*
of the facts.

That which we seek in things, over and above what is given to
us immediately, splits our entire being into two parts. We become

aware of standing in opposition to the world, as independent beings. The universe appears to us as two opposites: *I* and *world*.

47. Have you ever felt really separate from the world? Different? Alone? What is that like?

We set up this barrier between the world and ourselves as soon as consciousness lights up within us. But we never lose the feeling that we do belong to the world, that a link exists that connects us to it, that we are creatures not *outside*, but within, the universe.

This feeling engenders an effort to bridge the opposition. And, in the final analysis, the whole spiritual striving of humankind consists in bridging this opposition. The history of spiritual life is a continual searching for the unity between the "I" and the world. Religion, art, and science share this as their goal. The *religious believer* seeks the solution to the world-riddle posed by the "I," which is unsatisfied by the merely phenomenal world, in the revelation meted out by God. *Artists* try to incorporate the ideas of their "I" in various materials to reconcile what lives within them to the outer world. They, too, feel unsatisfied with the merely phenomenal world and seek to build into it the something more that their "I"-being, going above and beyond the world of phenomena, contains. *Thinkers* seek the laws of phenomena, striving to penetrate in thinking what they experience through observation. Only when we have made the *world content* into our *thought content* do we rediscover the connection from which we have sundered ourselves.

48. Have you ever used one of the arts to connect "world content" to "thought content" to establish or reestablish a connection to the world (i.e., a landscape painting, nature journaling, and so on)?

Dualism directs its gaze solely to the separation that human consciousness effects between the "I" and the world. Its whole effort is a futile struggle to reconcile these opposites, which it may call *spirit* and *matter*, *subject* and *object*, or *thinking* and *phenomenon*. It feels that a bridge between the two worlds must exist, but it is incapable of finding it. When human beings experience themselves as "I," they can do no other than think of this "I" as being on the side of *spirit*. When they then oppose the world to this "I," they ascribe to the world the perceptual realm ascribed to the senses: the *material* world. In this way, human beings place themselves within the opposition of spirit and matter. They do so all the more because their own bodies belong to the material world. The "I" thus belongs to the spiritual, as a part of it; while *material* things and processes, which are perceived by the senses, belong to the "world." All the riddles, therefore, that have to do with spirit and matter must be rediscovered by human beings in the fundamental riddle of their own essential being. *Monism* directs its gaze exclusively to unity, and seeks to deny or erase the opposites, present though these are.

Monism, until now, has attempted three solutions: either it denies spirit and becomes materialism; or it denies matter, seeking salvation through spiritualism; or else it claims that matter and spirit are inseparably united even in the simplest entity, so that it should come as no surprise if these two forms of existence, which after all are never apart, appear together in human beings.

Materialism can never offer a satisfactory explanation of the world. For every attempt at an explanation must begin with one's forming *thoughts* about phenomena. Thus, materialism starts with the *thought* of matter or of material processes. In so doing, it already has two different kinds of facts on hand: the material world and thoughts about it. Materialism attempts to understand the latter by seeing them as a purely material process. It believes that thinking occurs in the brain in the same way as digestion occurs in the animal organism. Just as it ascribes mechanical and organic effects to matter, materialism also assigns to matter the capacity, under certain circumstances, to think. But it forgets that all it has done is to shift the problem to another location. Materialists ascribe the capacity to think to matter rather than to themselves. And this brings them back to the starting point. How does matter manage to think about its own existence? Why does it not simply go on existing, perfectly content with itself? Materialism turns aside from the specific subject, our own "I"-being, and arrives at an unspecific, hazy configuration: matter. Here the same riddle comes up again. The materialist view can only displace the problem, not solve it.

49. Where do you see materialism in today's world? Why do people today seem to care so much about "things"?

And what of the spiritualist view? Pure *spiritualists* deny matter any independent existence and conceive of it only as a product of spirit. If they apply this view to the riddle of their own human existence, they are driven into a corner. In contrast to the "I," which may be placed on the side of spirit, the sensory world suddenly appears. No *spiritual* point of entry into it seems open; it has to be perceived and experienced by the "I" through material processes. As long as it tries to explain itself solely as a spiritual entity, the "I" cannot find such material processes within itself. What it works out for itself spiritually never contains the sensory world. Just as it is impossible for the materialist to declare spirit out of existence, so the spiritualist cannot disavow the external material world.

*50. Have you ever experienced the opposite of material-
ism, people who disavow the material world in the name
of spiritualism?*

To be sure, we have torn ourselves away from nature, but
we must still have taken something with us into our own being.
We must seek out this natural being within ourselves, and then
we shall also rediscover the connection to her. Dualism fails to
do this. It considers the inner human as a spiritual being, quite
foreign to nature, and then seeks to attach this being to nature.
No wonder that it cannot find the connecting link. We can only
find nature outside us if we first know her *within* us. What is
akin to her within us will be our guide. Our way is thus mapped
out for us. We do not wish to speculate about the interaction
of nature and spirit. We wish to descend into the depths of our
own being, to find there those elements that we have saved in
our flight out of nature.

The investigation of our own being must bring us the solution
to the riddle. We must come to a point where we can say to ourselves: Here I am no longer merely "I." There is something here
that is more than "I."

3. THINKING IN THE SERVICE
OF UNDERSTANDING THE WORLD

Insofar as we are conscious of it, *observation* and *thinking* are the two points of departure for all human spiritual striving.

No matter what principle we wish to establish, we must show either that we have observed it somewhere or we must express it in the form of a clear thought that anyone can rethink.

Our thinking about a horse and the object horse are two things that arise separately for us. And the object is accessible to us only through observation. Merely staring at a horse does not enable us to produce the concept *horse*, and neither will mere thinking bring forth the corresponding object. Chronologically, observation precedes even thinking, since we can become aware of thinking, too, only through observation.

Thinking differs essentially, as an object of observation, from all other things. The observation of a table or a tree occurs for me as soon as the objects enter the horizon of my experience. But I do not observe my thinking about the objects at the same time as I observe them. I observe the table, and I carry out my thinking about the table, but I do not observe that thinking in the same moment as my observation of the table. If I want to observe, along with the table, my thinking about the table, I must first take up a standpoint outside my own activity. While observation of objects and processes, and thinking about them, are both everyday situations that fill my ongoing life, *the observation of thinking* is a kind of exceptional state.

It is part of the peculiar nature of thinking that it is an activity directed only to the observed object, and not to the thinker. This is clear from how we express our thoughts about a thing, compared to how we express our feelings or acts of will. If I see an object and recognize it as a table, I do not generally say "I am thinking about a table," but rather "This is a table." Yet I could certainly say, "I am pleased with the table." In the first case, I am not concerned with communicating that I have entered into a relationship with the table; but in the second case it is precisely this relationship that is significant. Furthermore, with the statement, "I am thinking about a table," I have already entered into the exceptional state mentioned above, in which I make into an object of observation something that is always contained within my spiritual activity but not as an observed object.

This is the characteristic nature of thinking. The thinker forgets thinking while doing it. What concerns the thinker is not thinking, but the observed object of thinking. Hence the first observation that we make about thinking is that it is the unobserved element in our normal spiritual life. In other words, when I think, I do not look at my thinking, which I myself am producing, but at the object of thinking, which I am not producing.

I am in the same situation even if I allow the exceptional state of affairs to occur and think about my thinking itself. I can never observe my present thinking; only after I have thought can I take the experiences I have had during my thinking process as the object of my thinking. If I wanted to observe my present thinking, I would have to split myself into two personalities, one that thinks and one that looks on during this thinking, which I cannot do. I can observe my present thinking only in two separate acts.

Observation tells me that nothing guides me in combining my thoughts except the content of my thoughts. I am not guided by the material processes in my brain.

Most people today find it hard to grasp the concept of thinking in its purity. Whoever immediately counters the view of thinking developed here with the statement of Cabanis, that "the brain secretes thoughts as the liver does gall or the salivary ducts saliva" simply does not know what I am talking about. But for everyone who has the capacity to observe thinking—and, with good will, every normally constituted human being has this capacity—the observation of thinking is the most important observation that can be made. For in thinking we observe something of which we ourselves are the producers. We find ourselves facing something that to begin with is not foreign to us, but our own activity. We know how the thing we are observing comes about. We see through the relationships and the connections.

51. Have you ever tried to observe your thinking? If so, what is it like? Is it possible to be both an observer and a participant?

When we make thinking into an object of observation, we add to the rest of the observed world-content something that normally escapes our attention, but we do not change the way in which we relate to it, which is the same as to other things. We increase the number of the objects of our observation, but not our method of observing.

Without a doubt, in thinking we hold a corner of the world process where we must be present if anything is to occur. And this is exactly the point at issue. This is exactly why things stand over against me so puzzlingly: because I am so uninvolved in their creation. I simply find them present. But in the case of thinking, I know how it is done. This is why, for the contemplation of the whole world-process, there is no more primal starting point than thinking.

I contemplate the rest of the world with the help of thinking. Why should I make an exception for my thinking?

I believe I have now justified beginning my consideration of the world with thinking.

Before anything else can be understood, thinking must be understood.

It is the "I" itself that—*within* thinking—observes *its own* activity.

4. THE WORLD AS PERCEPT

*C*oncepts and *ideas* arise through thinking. Words cannot say what a concept is. Words can only make us notice that we have concepts. When we see a tree, our thinking reacts to our observation, a conceptual counterpart joins the object, and we consider the object and the conceptual counterpart as belonging together. When the object disappears from our field of observation, only the conceptual counterpart remains. The latter is the concept of the object. The wider our experience extends, the greater the sum of our concepts. But the concepts by no means stand apart from one another. They combine into a lawful whole. For example, the concept "organism" combines with others, such as "lawful development" and "growth." Other concepts, formed from individual things, collapse wholly into a unity. Thus, all concepts that I form about lions combine into the general concept "lion." In this way, individual concepts link together into a closed conceptual system, in which each has its particular place. Ideas are not qualitatively different from concepts. They are only concepts with more content—more saturated and more inclusive. I emphasize here that it is important to note at this point that my point of departure is *thinking*, not *concepts* or *ideas,* which must first be gained by thinking.

When I hear a noise, I first seek the concept that fits this observation. Someone who thinks no more of it simply hears the noise and leaves it at that. But by thinking about it, it becomes clear to me that I must regard the noise as an effect. Only when I combine the concept of *effect* with the perception of the noise am I inclined to go beyond the individual observation itself and seek a *cause.* The concept of effect evokes that of cause, and I then seek the causative object, which I find in the form of a partridge. But I can never gain the concepts of cause and effect by mere observation, no matter how many cases I may observe. Observation calls forth thinking, and it is only the latter that shows me how to link one isolated experience with another.

For thinking, by its very nature, goes over and above what has been observed.

Human consciousness is the stage where concept and observation meet and are connected to one another. This is, in fact, what characterizes human consciousness. It is the mediator between thinking and observation. To the extent that human beings observe things, things appear as given; to the extent that human beings think, they experience themselves as active. They regard things as *objects*, and themselves as thinking *subjects*. Because they direct their thinking to what they observe, they are conscious of objects; because they direct their thinking toward themselves, they are conscious of themselves; they are *self-aware*.

The activity that human beings exercise as *thinking* beings is therefore not merely subjective, but it is a kind of activity that is neither subjective nor objective; it goes beyond both these concepts. I should never say that my individual subject thinks; rather, it lives by the grace of thinking. Thus, thinking is an element that leads me beyond myself and unites me with objects. But it separates me from them at the same time, by setting me over against them as subject.

Just this establishes the dual nature of the human being: we think, and our thinking embraces ourselves along with the rest of the world; but at the same time we must also, by means of thinking, define ourselves as *individuals* standing over against *things*.

52. *We are separate and yet through our thinking are united with objects and the world around us. Have you ever felt*

*alone even when in a crowd, or have you ever felt connected
to someone even when alone?*

We must imagine that a being with a fully developed human intelligence arises from nothing and confronts the world. What this being would be aware of, before it brought thinking into action, is the pure content of observation. The world would then reveal to this being only the pure, relation-less aggregate of *sensory objects*: colors, sounds, sensations of pressure, warmth, taste, and smell, and then feelings of pleasure and unpleasure. This aggregate is the content of pure, thought-free observation.

Because of shifting habits of speech, it seems necessary for me to come to an agreement with my reader on the use of a word that I must employ from now on. The word is *percept*. I will use the word "*percept*" to refer to "the immediate objects of sensation" mentioned above, insofar as the conscious subject knows these objects through observation. Thus, it is not the process of observation but the *object* of observation that I designate with this name.

The naive person considers percepts, as they first appear, to be things that have an existence quite independent of the human being in question. If we see a tree, we initially believe that the tree, in the form that we see it, with its various colors, etc., is standing there in the spot to which our gaze is directed. From this naive standpoint, if we see the Sun appear in the morning as a disc on the horizon and then follow the progress of this disc, we believe that all of this exists and occurs just as we observe it. We cling fast to this belief until we meet other percepts that contradict the first. The child, with no experience of distances, reaches for the Moon, and only when a second percept comes to contradict the first can the child correct what at first seemed real to it. Every extension in the sphere of my percepts makes

119

me correct my image of the world. This is evident in daily life, just as it is in the spiritual evolution of humankind. The ancient image of the relation of the Earth to the Sun and the other heavenly bodies had to be replaced by that of Copernicus, because the ancient image did not agree with new, previously unknown percepts. When Dr. Franz operated on someone born blind, the latter said that before his operation he had arrived through the sense of touch at a very different image of the size of objects. He had to correct his tactile percepts with his visual percepts.

Why are we compelled continually to correct our observations? A simple reflection provides the answer to this question. If I stand at the end of an avenue, the trees at the other end appear to me smaller and closer together than those where I am standing. My perceptual picture changes as I change the place from which I make my observations. Thus, the form in which the perceptual image confronts me depends on conditions determined not by the object but by me, the perceiver. The avenue does not care where I stand. But the image that I have of the avenue is fundamentally dependent on where I stand. In the same way, it makes no difference to the Sun and the solar system that human beings regard them just from the Earth. But the perceptual image of the heavens that presents itself to human beings is determined by their living on the Earth. This dependence of the perceptual image on our place of observation is the easiest kind of dependence to understand. The issue becomes more difficult when we realize the dependence of our perceptual world on our bodily and spiritual organization. The physicist shows that vibrations of the air are present in the space where we hear a sound, and that even the body in which we seek the source of the sound displays a vibrating movement in its parts. But we become aware of this movement as sound only if we have a normally constructed ear. Without this, the whole world would be forever silent for us. Physiology teaches us that there are some people who perceive nothing of the magnificent splendor of color surrounding us. Their perceptual picture shows only nuances of dark and light. Others fail to perceive only a specific color, such as red. Their image of the world lacks this hue, and is therefore actually different from that of the average human being. I should like to call the dependence of my perceptual image on my place of observation a "mathematical" one, and its dependence on my organization a "qualitative" one. The relative sizes and distances of my percepts are determined through the former; their quality through the latter. That I see a red surface as red—this qualitative determination—depends on the organization of my eye.

Initially, then, our perceptual images are subjective.

53. Have you ever met someone and formed an initial perception only to change your views of the person after accumulating more perceptions? Why is it important that we are able to change our subjective percepts of objects and people over time?

I do not perceive only other things; I also perceive myself. In contrast to the perceptual images that continually come and go, *I* am what remains. This, initially, is the content of my percept of myself. When I have other percepts, the percept of the *"I"* can always appear in my consciousness. However, when I am immersed in the perception of a given object, then for the time being I am conscious only of the latter. The percept of my self can be added to this. I am then not merely conscious of the object, but also of my personality, which stands over against the object and observes it. I not only see a tree, I also know that *I am* the one who sees it. Moreover, I realize that something goes on in me *while* I observe the tree. If the tree disappears from my view, a remnant of this process remains in my consciousness: an image of the tree. As I was observing, this image united itself with my self. My self is thereby enriched: its content has received a new element into itself. I call this element my *mental picture (Vorstellung)* of the tree. There would be no need to speak of *mental pictures* if I did not experience them in the percept of my self. In that case, percepts would come and go; I would let them pass by. It is only because I perceive my self, and notice that with every percept the content of my self also changes, that I find myself compelled to connect the observation of the object with my own changed state, and to speak of my mental picture.

I perceive mental pictures *in my self* in the same way that I perceive colors, sounds, and so forth *in other objects.* From this point of view, I can now make a distinction, calling these other objects that stand over against me the *outer world,* while designating the content of my self-percept as the *inner world.*

5. KNOWING THE WORLD

Let me clarify my point with an example. When I throw a stone horizontally through the air, I see it in different places in succession. I connect these places along a line. In mathematics, I come to know various kinds of lines, among them the parabola. I know the parabola to be a line that results when a point moves in a certain lawful way. If I investigate the conditions according to which the thrown stone moves, I find that the line of its movement is identical with what I know as a parabola. That the stone moves precisely in a parabola is a consequence of the given conditions, and follows necessarily from them. The parabolic form belongs to the whole phenomenon, like all its other aspects. The spirit described above, which has no need of the detour of thinking, would take as given not only the sum of visual sensations in various places but also, united with the phenomenon, the parabolic form of the trajectory that *we* only add to the phenomenon by means of thinking.

It is not due to the objects that they are initially given to us without the corresponding concepts but to our spiritual organization. Our whole being functions in such a way that for everything in reality, the elements flow to us from two sides—from the side of *perceiving* and from the side of *thinking*.

Our thinking, unlike our sensing and feeling, is not individual. It is universal. Only because it is related to the individual's feeling and sensing does it receive an individual stamp in each separate human being. Human beings differentiate themselves from one another through these particular colorations of universal thinking. There is only one concept "triangle." It makes no difference to the content of this concept whether it is grasped by A or B—by this or that human carrier of consciousness. But each bearer of consciousness will grasp it in an individual way.

> 54. We grasp things in an individual way and yet it is possible to achieve a kind of universality through our thinking (triangle). What are the social implications of this dynamic?

The urge for knowledge arises in us because thinking in us reaches out beyond our separateness and relates itself to universal world existence. Beings without thinking do not have this urge. If other things confront them, no questions arise. Other things remain external to such beings. For thinking beings, a concept arises from the encounter with an external thing. The concept is that part of a thing that we do not receive from without, but from within. *Knowledge, cognition* is meant to accomplish the balance or union of the two elements, inner and outer.

A percept, then, is not something finished or closed off. It is one side of the total reality. The other side is the concept. The act of knowing (cognition) is the synthesis of percept and concept. Only percept and concept together make up the whole thing.

Thinking brings this content to the percept out of the human being's world of concepts and ideas. In contrast to perceptual content, which is given us from without, thought-content appears within. We shall call the form in which thought-content first arises *intuition*. Intuition is to thinking as *observation* is to perception. Intuition and observation are the sources of our knowledge.

> 55. Intuition and observation are the sources of our knowledge. When you make decisions, do you tend to do so based mostly on observations (sense impressions) or on intuition (from within)? Both ways of knowing are valid (Aristotle and Plato) but most of us tend to prefer one way or the other. The aim of this presentation by Steiner is for us to work holistically, using both the phenomena and our intuitive capacities in support of thinking.

To *explain* a thing, to *make it comprehensible*, means nothing other than to place it into the context from which it has been torn by the arrangement of our organization.

What meets us in observation as separate details is linked, item by item, through the coherent, unitary world of our intuitions. Through thinking we join together into one everything that we separated through perceiving.

6. HUMAN INDIVIDUALITY

The moment a percept emerges on the horizon of my observation, thinking, too, is activated in me. An element of my thought system—a specific intuition, a concept—unites with the percept. Then, when the percept disappears from my field of vision, what remains? What remains is my intuition, with its relationship to the specific percept that formed in the moment of perceiving. How vividly I can then later represent this relationship to myself depends upon how my spiritual and bodily organism is functioning. A *mental picture* is nothing but an intuition related to a specific percept. It is a concept, once linked to a percept, for which the relation to that percept has remained. My concept of a lion is not formed *out of* my percepts of lions. Yet my mental picture of a lion is certainly formed by means of perception. I can convey the concept of a lion to those who have never seen a lion. But without their own perceiving, I will not succeed in conveying a vivid mental picture.

A *mental picture*, then, is an individualized concept. We can now understand how mental pictures can represent the things of reality for us. The full reality of a thing is revealed to us in the moment of observation, out of the merging of a concept and a percept. Through a percept, the concept receives an individualized form, a relationship to that specific percept. The concept survives in us in this individual form, with its characteristic relationship to the percept, and forms the mental picture of the corresponding thing. If we encounter a second thing and the same concept combines itself with it, then we recognize it as belonging to the same species as the first, for we find not only a corresponding concept in our conceptual system, but the individualized concept with its characteristic relationship to this same object, and we recognize the object once again. Thus, a mental picture stands between a percept and a concept. A mental picture is the specific concept that points to the percept.

> *56. We form mental pictures that connect our perceptions and our concepts. If a person has formed a concept that is a stereotype (concerning race, gender, religion, etc.), how can the methodology described in this chapter help to correct these erroneous mental pictures?*

The sum of everything of which I can form mental pictures I can call my "experience." Hence, the greater the number of individualized concepts a person has, the richer their experience will be. A person lacking intuitive capacity, on the other hand, is unsuited to acquire experience. For such a person, once objects are out of sight they are lost, because the concepts that ought to be brought into relationship with them are lacking. A person whose capacity to think is well developed but who perceives poorly because of coarse sensory equipment will be equally incapable of gathering experience. Such persons might acquire concepts somehow, but their intuitions will lack a vivid relationship to specific things. A thoughtless traveler and a scholar living in abstract conceptual systems are equally unable to have rich experience.

> *57. How can we work to achieve a balance between the two extremes described in the above sentences?*

Thinking and *feeling* correspond to the dual nature of our being, on which we have already reflected. *Thinking* is the element through which we participate in the universal process of the cosmos; *feeling* is the element through which we can withdraw into the confines of our own being.

Our thinking unites us with the world; our feeling leads us back into ourselves and makes us individuals. If we were only thinking and perceiving beings, then our whole life would flow past in monotonous indifference. If we could only *know* ourselves as selves, then we would be completely indifferent to ourselves. It is only because we have self-feeling along with self-cognition, and pleasure and pain along with the perception of things, that we live as individual beings whose existence is not limited to our conceptual relation to the rest of the world, but who also have a special value for ourselves. Some might be tempted to see in the life of feeling an element more richly imbued with reality than thinking contemplation of the world. The reply to this is that the life of feeling has this richer meaning only for my individuality. For the world as a whole, my feeling life can attain value only if the feeling, as a percept of my self, combines with a concept and so integrates itself indirectly into the cosmos.

Our life is a continual oscillation between our individual existence and living with the universal world process. The farther we rise into the universal nature of thinking, where what is individual continues to interest us only as an example, an instance of a concept, the more we let go of our character as particular entities—as completely specific, separate personalities. The more we descend into the depths of our own life, allowing our feelings to resonate with the experiences of the outer world, the more we separate ourselves from universal being. A true individual will be the person who reaches highest, with his or her feelings, into the region of ideals. There are people for whom even the most universal ideas entering their heads still retain a special coloring that shows them unmistakably connected with their bearer. There are others whose concepts meet us so completely without trace of ownership as to seem unconnected to anyone of flesh and blood.

Making mental pictures already gives our conceptual life an individual stamp. After all, each of us has a standpoint from which to view the world. Our concepts connect themselves to our percepts. We think universal concepts in our own special way. This characteristic quality is a result of our standpoint in the world, of the sphere of perception connected to our place in life.

In contrast to this particularity is another, dependent on our individual constitution. How we are constituted, after all, makes for a special, well-defined entity. We each connect special feelings with our percepts, and do so in the most varying degrees of intensity. This is the individual aspect of our personality. It remains left over after we have accounted for the specificities of the stage on which we act out our lives.

A feeling-life completely devoid of thought must gradually lose all connection with the world. Yet for human beings, oriented as they are toward wholeness, knowledge of things will go hand in hand with education and development of the life of feeling.

Feeling is the means by which concepts first gain concrete *life*.

58. Given Steiner's statement that "a true individual reaches... highest, with his or her feelings, into the region of ideals," can you describe situations when you have acted on the basis of an ideal or value and a feeling of love for that ideal?

7. ARE THERE LIMITS TO COGNITION?

59. Before reading further, what is your initial take on this question: Are there limits to knowledge?

We have established that the elements needed to explain reality are to be drawn from the two spheres of perceiving and thinking. As we have seen, we are so organized that the full, total reality (including that of ourselves as subjects) initially appears to us as a duality. Cognition overcomes this duality by composing the thing as a whole out of the two elements of reality: the percept, and the concept worked out by thinking. Let us call the way in which the world meets us, before it has gained its true form through cognition, "the world of appearance," in contrast to the unified reality composed of percepts and concepts. We can then say that the world is given to us as a duality, and cognition assimilates it into a (monistic) unity. A philosophy that proceeds from this fundamental principal can be characterized as monistic philosophy or *monism*. In contrast to it stands two-world theory or *dualism*. The latter does not, for example, assume that there are two sides to a unitary reality that are separated merely by our organization, but that there are two worlds that are absolutely distinct from one another. Dualism then seeks the explanatory principles for one world in the other.

Dualism rests on a false conception of what we call cognition. It separates the whole of existence into two regions, each of which has its own laws, and lets those regions confront one another outwardly.

Dualism mistakenly transfers the contrast between objects and subjects, which has meaning only within the perceptual realm, to purely imagined entities outside this realm. But things separated in the perceptual field are separate only as long as the perceiver refrains from thinking—for thinking suspends all separation and reveals it to be merely subjective.

For naive consciousness, the self-sufficient existence of what can be experienced through ideas is not considered to be real in the same way as what can be experienced through the senses.

Naive consciousness demands revelation through means accessible to sensory perception. God must appear bodily, and the testimony of thinking counts little. Rather, divinity must be confirmable by the senses through such things as the transformation of water into wine.

The metaphysical realist may object to the monist: "As far as your organism is concerned, it may be that your cognition is perfect in itself, that it lacks nothing; but you do not know how the world would be reflected in an intelligence organized differently from your own." To this monism will respond: "If there are non-human intelligences whose percepts have a form different from our own, what has meaning for me is still only what reaches me through my perceiving and concepts."

Readers will see from what has been said, but still more so from what will be said later, that everything both sensory *and* *spiritual* that meets a human being is here taken to be a "percept" until it is grasped by the actively elaborated concept. "Senses" of the kind normally meant by the word are not necessary to have percepts of soul or spirit.

> *60. In the previous paragraphs, Rudolf Steiner describes various ways of knowing the world: the dualist, the naïve realist, and so on. Have you known people who show these tendencies (or are these terms just archaic philosophical descriptors)?*

8. THE FACTORS OF LIFE

A mystical view based solely on feeling errs in wanting to experience what it ought to know; it wants to make something that is individual, feeling, into something universal.

Feeling is a purely individual act. It is a relationship of the outer world to our subject, insofar as that relationship finds expression in a purely subjective experience. Through it's thinking, the "I" participates in general, universal life. Through thinking, it relates percepts to itself, and itself to percepts, in a purely conceptual way; in feeling, it experiences a relationship of the object to its subject. But in willing, the reverse is the case. In willing, too, we have a percept before us: namely, that of the individual relation of our self to what is objective. And whatever is not a purely conceptual factor in our will is just as much a mere object of perception as anything in the outer world.

> 61. Thinking, feeling, willing... these are three crucial aspects of our soul life. Which do you tend to use most frequently? Do you try and first understand things, or experience things through feelings, or take action?

Whoever turns toward essential thinking finds within it both feeling and will, and both of these in the depths of their reality. Whoever turns aside from thinking toward "pure" feeling and willing loses the true reality of feeling and willing. If we experience thinking intuitively, we also do justice to the experience of feeling and will.

9. THE IDEA OF FREEDOM

To observe thinking is to live, during the observation, immediately within the weaving of a self-supporting spiritual entity. We could even say that whoever wants to grasp the essence of the spirit in the form in which it first presents itself to human beings can do so in the self-sustaining activity of thinking.

But, if we see what is really present in thinking, we will recognize that only one part of reality is present in the percept and that we experience the other part—which belongs to it and is necessary for it to appear as full reality—in the permeation of the percept by thinking. We shall then see, in what appears in consciousness as thinking, not a shadowy copy of reality, but a spiritual essence that sustains itself. Of this spiritual essence we can say that it becomes present to our consciousness through intuition. Intuition is the conscious experience, within what is purely spiritual, of a purely spiritual content. The essence of thinking can be grasped only through intuition.

The effective essence in thinking has a double function. First, it represses the human organization's own activity and, second, it replaces that activity with itself. Even the first of these, the repression of the bodily organization, is a result of thinking activity—of the part of that activity that prepares the appearance of thinking. We can see from this in what sense thinking is reflected in the bodily organization. Once we see this, we will no longer be able to mistake the significance of that reflection and take it for thinking itself. If we walk over softened ground, our footsteps dig into the earth. We are not tempted to say that the footprints are driven upward from below by forces in the ground. We will not attribute to those forces any share in the origin of the footprints. Similarly, if we observe the essence of thinking without prejudice, we will not attribute any part of this essence to traces in the bodily organism that arise because thinking prepares its appearance by means of the body.

These are the elements to be considered in an act of will. The immediate mental picture or concept becomes a motive and determines the goal or purpose of my willing; my characterological disposition determines whether or not I will direct my activity toward that goal. The mental picture of taking a walk during the next half hour determines the goal of my activity. This mental picture, however, is elevated into a motive of willing only if it encounters a suitable characterological disposition; that is, if in my life to date I have developed mental pictures of, for example, the usefulness of taking walks and the value of health and, further, if the mental picture of taking walks is linked in me with feelings of pleasure.

Thus, we must distinguish between (1) the possible subjective dispositions that are suited to making specific mental pictures and concepts into motives and (2) the possible mental pictures and concepts that are capable of influencing my characterological disposition so that an act of will results. The former represent the motive powers, the latter the goals of morality.

The second sphere of human life is feeling. Particular feelings accompany percepts of the external world. These feelings can become motive powers for action. If I see a hungry person, my compassion can form the motive power to act. Such feelings include shame, pride, sense of honor, humility, remorse, compassion, vengeance, gratitude, piety, loyalty, love, and duty.

Finally, the third level of life is thinking and mental picturing. Through mere reflection, a mental picture or concept can become a motive for action. Mental pictures become motives because, in the course of life, we constantly link certain goals of our will to percepts that recur repeatedly in more or less modified form. Therefore, people who are not without experience are always aware, along with certain percepts, of mental pictures of actions they themselves have performed or seen others perform in similar cases. These mental pictures float before them as defining patterns for all later decisions; they become part of their characterological disposition. We can call this motive power of the will practical experience. Practical experience merges gradually into purely tactful action.

If we act under the influence of intuitions, then the motive power of our action is pure thinking.

The principle of producing through one's actions the greatest amount of pleasure for oneself—that is, of attaining individual happiness—is called egoism. This individual happiness is sought either through thinking ruthlessly only of one's own welfare and striving for it even at the expense of the happiness of other individuals (pure egoism), or through promoting the good of others because one hopes for indirect advantages from their happiness, or through fear of endangering one's own interests by harming others.

62. Why do you think so many people today are self-centered and egoistic?

A special kind of moral principle is involved when the commandment does not announce itself to us through outer authority, but from within ourselves. We may call this moral autonomy. We then hear within ourselves the voice to which we must submit. The expression of this voice is conscience.

People vary in their capacity for intuition. For one person, ideas just bubble up, while another achieves them by much labor. The situations in which people live, and which serve as the scene of their activity, are no less varied. How I act will therefore depend on how my capacity for intuition works in relation to a particular situation. The sum of ideas active within us, the real content of our intuitions, constitutes what is individual in each of us, notwithstanding the universality of the world of ideas. To the extent that the intuitive content turns into action, it is the ethical content of the individual. Allowing this intuitive content to live itself out fully is the highest driving force of morality. At the same time, it is the highest motive of those who realize that, in the end, all other moral principles unite within it. We can call this standpoint ethical individualism.

Humans are free to the extent that they are able to obey themselves at each instant of their lives. An ethical deed is only my deed if it can be called a free deed in this sense.

> 63. How is this portrayal of ethics and morality different from what has historically come more from organized religion? Can you think of actions you have performed on the basis of an intuition, in which you have united the fourth level of motive power and motive?

To act out of freedom does not exclude moral laws, but rather includes them. Still, it stands on a higher level than action dictated by moral laws alone. Why should my action serve the welfare of the whole any less if I have acted out of love than if I acted only because I feel a duty to serve the welfare of the whole? The simple concept of duty excludes freedom, because duty does not recognize individuality but demands instead subjection of individuality to a general norm. Freedom of action is thinkable only from the standpoint of ethical individualism.

> 64. But how is it possible for humans to live together socially if everyone is striving merely to express his or her own individuality?

To live in love of action, and to let live in understanding of the other's will, is the fundamental maxim of free human beings.

Only because individuals are of one spirit can they live out their lives side by side. A free person lives in trust that the other free person belongs to the same spiritual world and that they will concur with each other in their intentions. Those who are free demand no *agreement* from their fellows, but they expect it, because it is inherent in human nature. This is not meant to indicate the necessity of this or that outer arrangement. Rather, it is meant to indicate the attitude, the state of the soul, with which a human being, experiencing himself or herself amidst esteemed fellow human beings, can best do justice to human dignity.

Our life is made up of free and unfree actions. Yet we cannot think the concept of the human through to the end without arriving at the free spirit as the purest expression of human nature. Indeed, we are only truly human to the extent that we are free.

As a perceptual object, I am subject to continual transformation. As a child I was one thing, as a youth another, as an adult still another. In fact, at every moment the perceptual picture of myself is different from what it was a moment before. These changes can take place in such a way that the same person (the stereotypical human) is always expressed in them or in such a way that they represent the expression of the free spirit. My actions, too, as objects of perception, are subject to such changes.

There is a possibility for the human perceptual object to transform itself, just as within the plant seed there lies the possibility of becoming a whole plant. The plant will transform itself because of the objective lawfulness lying within it. Humans remain in an incomplete state if they do not take in hand the transformative substance within themselves, and transform themselves through their own power. Nature makes human beings merely natural creatures; society makes them law-abiding actors; but they can only make themselves into free beings.

> *65. How is the preceding picture of freedom different from what is usually understood as "freedom"?*

12. MORAL IMAGINATION (DARWINISM AND ETHICS)

Imagination is the chief means by which human beings produce concrete mental pictures from the sum of their ideas. Free
spirits need moral imagination to realize their ideas and make
them effective. Moral imagination is the source of a free spirit's
actions. Therefore, only people who have moral imagination are
really morally productive.

To turn a mental picture into a reality, moral imagination
must set to work in a specific field of percepts. Human action
does not create percepts, it recasts already-existing percepts and
gives them a new form. To be able to transform a specific perceptual object or group of objects in accordance with a moral mental
picture, one must have understood the laws of the perceptual picture to which one wants to give new form or new direction—that
is, one must have understood how it has worked until now.

> 66. Innovation is often more about improving existing reali-
> ties than it is about discovering something totally different.
> For instance, we have had telephones for many years, but
> the iPhone involved "recasting" something that already
> exists into a new form. For that, Steve Jobs and others
> needed new mental pictures, new imaginations. What can
> education do to foster creative imagination?

The capacity to transform the world of percepts is moral technique. It is learnable in the sense that any knowledge is learnable. Generally, people are better equipped to find concepts for
the world that are already finished than to determine produc-
tively, out of their imagination, future, not-yet-existent actions.
Therefore, those without moral imagination may well receive
the moral mental pictures of other people and skillfully work
them into reality. The reverse can also occur: people with moral

imagination can lack technical skill and may have to make use of others to realize their mental pictures.

67. Have you ever been in a group or team in which it was clear that some members were better at imagination, and others were better with the technical skills needed to get a job done?

To be free means: to be able—on my own, through moral imagination—to determine the mental pictures (motives) underlying an action. Freedom is impossible if something outside myself (whether a mechanical process or a merely inferred, otherworldly God) determines my moral mental pictures. Therefore, I am free only when I produce these mental pictures myself, not merely when I can carry out motives that another has placed within me. Free beings are those who can will what they themselves hold to be right.

68. How do you relate to this view of human freedom?

Practical Training in Thought

Rudolf Steiner, lecture in Karlsruhe, January 18, 1909

It may seem strange that an anthroposophist should feel called upon to speak about practical training in thought, since there is a widespread opinion that Anthroposophy is highly impractical and has no connection with life. Such a view could arise only among those who see things superficially. In reality, what we are concerned with here can guide us in the most ordinary affairs of everyday life. It is something that can be transformed at any moment into sensation and feeling, enabling us to meet life with assurance and to acquire a firm position in it.

Many people who call themselves practical imagine that their actions are guided by the most practical principles. But if we inquire more closely, we find that their so-called practical thought is often not thought at all but only the continuing pursuit of traditional opinions and habits. An entirely objective observation of the "practical" person's thought and an examination of what is usually termed "practical thinking" will reveal the fact that it generally contains little that can be called practical. What to them is known as practical thought or thinking consists in following the example of some authority whose ideas are accepted as a standard in the construction of some object. Anyone who thinks differently is considered impractical because this thought does not coincide with traditional ideas.

When something really practical has been invented, it has often been done by a person without practical knowledge of that particular subject. Take, for instance, the modern postage stamp. It would be most natural to assume that it was invented by some practical post office official. It was not. At the beginning of the last century it was a complicated affair to mail a letter. In order to dispatch a letter one had to go to the nearest receiving office where various books had to be referred to and many other formalities complied with. The uniform rate of postage known today is hardly sixty years old, and our present postage stamp that makes this possible was not invented by a practical postal employee at all but by someone completely outside the post office. This was the Englishman, Rowland Hill.

After the uniform system of postage stamps had been devised, the English minister who was then in charge of the mail declared in Parliament that one could not assume any simplification of the system would increase the volume of mail as the impractical Hill anticipated. Even if it did, the London post office would be entirely inadequate to handle the increased volume. It never occurred to this highly "practical" individual that the post office must be fitted to the amount of business, not the business to the size of the post office. Indeed, in the shortest possible time this idea, which an "impractical" man had to defend against a "practical" authority, became a fact. Today, stamps are used everywhere as a matter of course for sending letters.

It was similar with the railroads. In 1837, when the first railroad in Germany was to be built, the members of the Bavarian College of Medicine were consulted on the advisability of the project and they voiced the opinion that it would be unwise to build railroads. They added that if this project were to be carried out, then at least a high board fence would have to be erected on both sides of the line to protect the public from possible brain and nervous shock.

When the railroad from Potsdam to Berlin was planned, Postmaster General Stengler said, "I am now dispatching two stagecoaches daily to Potsdam and these are never full. If people are determined to throw their money out the window, they can do it much more simply without building a railroad!"

But the real facts of life often sweep aside the "practical," that is to say, those who believe in their own ability to be practical. We must clearly distinguish between genuine thinking and so-called "practical thinking" that is merely reasoning in traditional ruts of thought.

As a starting point to our consideration I will tell you of an experience I had during my student days. A young colleague once came to me glowing with the joy of one who has just hit upon a really clever idea, and announced that he must go at once to see Professor X (who at the time taught machine construction at the University), for he had just made a great discovery. "I have discovered," he said, "how, with a small amount of steam power and by simply rearranging the machinery, an enormous amount of work can be done by one machine." He was in such a rush to see the professor that this was all he could tell me. He failed to find him, however, so he returned and explained the whole matter to me. It all smacked of perpetual motion, but after all, why shouldn't even that be possible? After I had listened to his explanation I had to tell him that although his plan undoubtedly appeared to be cleverly thought out, it was a case that might be compared in practice with that of a person who, on boarding a railway car, pushes with all his might and then believes when it moves that he has actually started it. "That," I said to him, "is the thought principle underlying your discovery." Finally, he saw it himself and did not return to the professor.

It is thus quite possible to shut ourselves up within a shell fashioned by our own thoughts. In rare cases this can be observed distinctly, but there are many similar examples in life that do not always reach such a striking extreme as the one just cited. Someone who is able to study human nature more intimately, however, knows that a large number of thought processes are of this kind and often sees, we might say, people standing in the car pushing it from within and believing that they are making it move. Many of the events of life would take a different course if people did not so often try to solve their problems by thus deluding themselves.

True practice in thinking presupposes a right attitude and a proper feeling for thinking. How can a right attitude toward thinking be attained? Anyone who believes that thought is merely an activity that takes place within the head or the soul cannot have the right feeling for thought. Whoever harbors this idea will be constantly diverted by a false feeling from seeking right habits of thought and from making the necessary demands on thinking. A person who would acquire the right feeling for thought must say, "If I can formulate thoughts about things, and learn to understand them through thinking, then these things themselves must first have contained these thoughts. The things must have been built up according to these thoughts, and only because this is so can I in turn extract these thoughts from the things."

It can be imagined that this world outside and around us may be regarded in the same way as a watch. The comparison between the human organism and a watch is often used, but those who make it frequently forget the most important point. They forget the watchmaker. The fact must be kept clearly in mind that the wheels have not united and fitted themselves together of their own accord and thus made the watch "go," but that first there was the watchmaker who put the different parts of the watch together. The watchmaker must never be forgotten. Through thoughts the watch has come into existence. The thoughts have flowed, as it were, into the watch, into the thing.

The works and phenomena of nature must be viewed in a similar way. In the works of human beings it is easy to picture this to ourselves, but with the works of nature it is not so easily done. Yet these, too, are the result of spiritual activities and behind them are spiritual beings. Thus, when a person thinks about things he or she only re-thinks what is already in them. The belief that the world has been created by thought and is still ceaselessly being created in this manner is the belief that can alone fructify the actual inner practice of thought.

It is always the denial of the spiritual in the world that produces the worst kind of malpractice in thought, even in the field of science. Consider, for example, the theory that our planetary system arose from a primordial nebula that began to rotate and then densified into a central body from which rings and globes detached themselves, thus mechanically bringing into existence the entire solar system. Anyone who propounds this theory is committing a grave error of thought.

A simple experiment used to be made in the schools to demonstrate this theory. A drop of oil was made to float in a glass of water. The drop was then pierced with a pin and made to rotate. As a result, tiny globules of oil were thrown off from the central drop creating a miniature planetary system, thus proving to the pupil—so the teacher thought—that this planetary system could come into existence through a purely mechanical process.

Only impractical thinking can draw such conclusions from this little experiment, since those who would apply this theory to the cosmos have forgotten something that ordinarily might well be forgotten occasionally—themselves. They forget that they themselves have brought this whole thing into rotation. If they had not been there and conducted the whole experiment, the separation of the little globules from the large drop would never have occurred. Had this fact been observed and applied logically to the cosmic system, they then would have been using complete healthy thinking. Similar errors of thought play a great part especially in science. Such things are far more important than people generally believe.

Considering the real practice of thought, it must be realized that thoughts can only be drawn from a world in which they already exist. Just as water can only be taken from a glass that actually contains water, so thoughts can only be extracted from things within which these thoughts are concealed. The world is built by thought, and for this reason alone thought can be extracted from it. Were it otherwise, practical thought could not arise. When people can feel the full truth of these words, it will be easy for them to dispense with abstract thought. If they can confidently believe that thoughts are concealed behind the things around them, and that the actual facts of life take their course in obedience to thought—if they feel this, they will easily be converted to a practical habit of thinking based on truth and reality.

Let us now look at that practice of thinking that is of special importance to those who stand upon an anthroposophic foundation. The one who is convinced that the world of facts is born of thought will grasp the importance of the development of right thinking.

People who wish to fructify their thinking to such a degree that it will always take the right course in life must be guided by the following rules and must understand that these are actual, practical, and fundamental principles. If they will try again and again to shape their thinking according to these rules, certain effects will result. Their thinking will become practical even though at first it may not seem so. Other additional mental experiences of quite a different kind also will come to those who apply these fundamental principles.

They can begin by observing, as accurately as possible, something accessible in the outer world—for instance, the weather. They can watch the configuration of the clouds in the evening, the conditions at sunset, and so on, and mentally retain an exact picture of what has been observed. They should try to keep the picture in all its details before themselves for some time and endeavor to preserve as much of it as possible until the next day. At some time the next day they should again make a study of the weather conditions and again endeavor to gain an exact picture of them.

If in this manner they have pictured to themselves exactly the sequential order of the weather conditions, they will become distinctly aware that their thinking gradually becomes richer and more intense. For what makes thought impractical is the tendency to ignore details when observing a sequence of events in the world and to retain but a vague, general impression of them. What is of value, what is essential and fructifies thinking, is just this ability to form exact pictures, especially of successive events, so that one can say, "Yesterday it was like that; today it is like this." Thus, one calls up as graphically as possible an inner image of the two juxtaposed scenes that lie apart in the outer world.

This is, so to speak, nothing else but a certain expression of confidence in the thoughts that underlie reality. Those experimenting ought not to draw any conclusions immediately or to deduce from today's observation what kind of weather they might have tomorrow. That would corrupt their thinking. Instead, they must confidently feel that the things of outer reality are definitely related to one another and that tomorrow's events are somehow connected with those of today. But they must not speculate on these things. They must first inwardly re-think the sequence of the outer events as exactly as possible in mental pictures, and then place these images side by side, allowing them to melt into one another. This is a definite rule of thought that must be followed by those who wish to develop factual thinking. It is particularly advisable that this principle be practiced on those very things that are not yet understood and the inner connection of which has not yet been penetrated.

Therefore, researchers be confident that events that they do not yet understand (the weather, for instance) and that in the outer world are interconnected will lead to inner connections. This must be done only in images, while refraining from thinking. The person must say inwardly, "I do not yet know what the relation is, but I shall let these things grow within me and if I refrain from speculation they will bring something about in me." It can be readily believed that something may take place in the invisible members of a person's nature if exact inner images of succeeding events are formed and at the same time all thinking is restrained.

The vehicle of a human being's thought life is the astral body. As long as the human being is engaged in speculative thinking, this astral body is the slave of the "I." This conscious activity, however, does not occupy the astral body exclusively because the latter is also related in a certain manner to the whole cosmos.

Now, to the extent we restrain arbitrary thinking and simply form mental pictures of successive events, to that extent do the inner thoughts of the world act within us and imprint themselves, without our being aware of it, on our astral body. To the extent we insert ourselves into the course of the world through observation of the events in the world and receive these images into our thoughts with the greatest possible clarity, allowing them to work within us, to that extent do those members of our organism that are withdrawn from our consciousness become ever more intelligent. If, in the case of inwardly connected events, we have once acquired the faculty of letting the new picture melt into the preceding one in the same way that the transition occurred in nature, it shall be found after a time that our thinking has gained considerable flexibility.

This is the procedure to be followed in matters not yet understood. Things, however, that are understood—events of everyday life, for example—should be treated in a somewhat different manner.

Let us presume that someone, perhaps our neighbor, had done this or that. We think about it and ask ourselves why he did it. We decide he has perhaps done it in preparation for something he intends to do the next day. We do not go any further but clearly picture his act and try to form an image of what he may do, imagining that the next day he will perform such and such an act. Then we wait to see what he really does since he may or may not do what we expected of him. We take note of what does happen and correct our thoughts accordingly. Thus, events of the present are chosen that are followed in thought into the future. Then we wait to see what actually happens.

This can be done either with actions involving people or something else. Whenever something is understood, we try to form a thought picture of what in our opinion will take place. If our opinion proves correct, our thinking is justified and all is well. If, however, something different from our expectation occurs, we review our thoughts and try to discover our mistake. In this way we try to correct our erroneous thinking by calm observation and examination of our errors. An attempt is made to find the reason for things occurring as they did. If we are right, however, we must be especially careful not to boast of our prediction and say, "Oh well, I knew yesterday that this would happen!"

This is again a rule based upon confidence that there is an inner necessity in things and events, that in the facts themselves there slumbers something that moves things. What is thus working within these things from one day to another are thought forces, and we gradually become conscious of them when meditating on things. By such exercises these thought forces are called up into our consciousness and if what has been thus foreseen is fulfilled, we are in tune with them. We have then established an inner relation with the real thought activity of the matter itself. So we train ourselves to think, not arbitrarily, but according to the inner necessity and the inner nature of the things themselves.

But our thinking can also be trained in other directions. An occurrence of today is also linked to what happened yesterday. We might consider a naughty child, for example, and ask ourselves what may have caused this behavior. The events are traced back to the previous day and the unknown cause hypothesized by saying to ourselves, "Since this occurred today, I must believe that it was prepared by this or that event that occurred yesterday or perhaps the day before." We then find out what had actually occurred and thus discover whether or not our thought was correct. If the true cause has been found, very well, but if our conclusion was wrong, then we should try to correct the mistake, find out how our thought process developed, and how it ran its course in reality.

To practice these principles is the important point. Time must be taken to observe things as though we were inside the things themselves with our thinking. We should submerge ourselves in the things and enter into their inner thought activity. If this is done, we gradually become aware of the fact that we are growing together with things. We no longer feel that they are outside us and we are here inside our shell thinking about them. Instead we come to feel as if our own thinking occurred within the things themselves. When a person has succeeded to a high degree in doing this, many things will become clear.

Goethe was such a man. He was a thinker who always lived with his thought within the things themselves. In 1826, the psychologist Heinroth's book *Anthropology* characterized Goethe's thought as "objective." Goethe himself appreciated this characterization. What was meant is that such thinking does not separate itself from things, but remains within them. It moves within the necessity of things. Goethe's thinking was at the same time perception, and his perception was thinking. He had developed this way of thinking to a remarkable degree. More than once it occurred that, when he had planned to do something, he would go to the window and remark to the person who happened to be with him, "In three hours we shall have rain!" Therefore, it would happen. In the little patch of sky he could see from the window, he could forecast the weather for the next few hours. His true thinking, remaining within the objects, thus enabled him to sense the coming event preparing itself in the preceding one.

Much more can actually be accomplished through practical thinking than is commonly supposed. When people have made these principles of thinking their own, they will notice that their thinking really becomes practical, that their horizon widens, and that they can grasp the things of the world in quite a different way. Gradually their attitude toward things and other people will change completely. An actual process will take place within them that will alter their whole conduct. It is of immense importance that they try to grow into the things in this way with their thinking, for it is in the most eminent sense a practical undertaking to train one's thinking by such exercises.

There is another exercise that is to be practiced especially by those to whom the right idea usually does not occur at the right time.

Such people should try, above all, to stop their thinking from being forever influenced and controlled by the ordinary course of worldly events and all that comes with them. As a rule, when people lie down for half an hour of rest, their thoughts are allowed to play freely in a thousand different directions; or, on the other hand, they may become absorbed with some problem in life. Before they realize it, such things will have crept into their consciousness and claimed their whole attention. If this habit persists, such people will never experience a time when the right idea occurs to them at the right moment.

If they really want this to happen, whenever they can spare a half hour for rest, they must tell themselves, "Whenever I can spare the time, I will think about something that I have chosen and bring it into my consciousness arbitrarily of my own free will. For example, I will think of something that occurred two years ago during a walk. I will deliberately recall what occurred then, and I will think about it if for only five minutes. During those five minutes I will banish everything else from my mind and choose for myself the subject about which I wish to think."

We need not even choose a difficult a subject such as this one. The point is never to change one's mental process through difficult exercises, but to get away from the ordinary routine of life in one's thinking. We must think of something quite separate from what enmeshes us during the course of the ordinary day. If nothing occurs to us to think about, we may open a book at random and occupy our thoughts with whatever first catches our eye. Or we may choose to think of something we saw at a particular time that morning on the way to work and to which we might otherwise have ignored. The main point is that it should be something totally different from the ordinary run of daily events, something that would otherwise not have occupied our thoughts.

If such exercises are practiced systematically again and again, it will soon be noticed that ideas come at the right moments, and the right thoughts occur when needed.

Through these exercises thinking will become activated and mobile—something of immense importance in practical life.

Let us consider another exercise that is especially helpful in improving one's memory.

One tries at first in the crude way people usually recall past events to remember something that occurred, let us say, yesterday. Such recollections are, as a rule, indistinct and colorless, and most people are satisfied if they can just remember a person's name. But if it is desired to develop one's memory, one can no longer be content with this. This must be clear. The following exercise must be systematically practiced, saying to oneself, "I will recall exactly the man I saw yesterday, the street corner where I met him, and what happened to be in his vicinity. I will draw the whole picture as accurately as possible and will even imagine the color and cut of his coat and vest." Most people will find themselves utterly incapable of doing this and quickly see how much is lacking in their recollections to produce a really lifelike, graphic picture of what they met and experienced only yesterday.

Since this is true in the majority of cases, we must begin with that condition in which many people are unable to recollect their most recent experiences. It is only too true that most people's observations of things and events are usually inaccurate and vague. The results of a test given by a professor in one of the universities demonstrated that out of thirty students who took the test, only two had observed an occurrence correctly; the remaining twenty-eight reported it inaccurately. But a good memory is the child of accurate observation. A reliable memory is attained, let me repeat, by accurate observation and it can also be said that in a certain roundabout way of the soul it is born as the child of exact observation.

But what should people do if they cannot at first accurately remember their experiences of yesterday? First, they should try to remember as accurately as possible what actually occurred. When recollections fail, they should fill in the picture with something incorrect that was not really there. The main point is to complete the picture. Suppose it was forgotten whether a person was wearing a brown or a black coat. One might picture a brown coat and brown trousers with such and such buttons on a vest and a yellow necktie. One might further imagine a general situation in which there was a yellow wall, with a tall man passing on the left, a short one on the right, and so on.

Everything that can be remembered is put into the picture, and what cannot be remembered is added imaginatively to complete a mental picture. Of course, it is incorrect at first, but through the effort to create a complete picture we are induced to observe more accurately. Such exercises must be continued, and although we might try and fail fifty times, perhaps the fifty-first time we will be able to remember accurately what the person we have met looked like, the clothes, and even little details like the buttons on a vest. Then nothing will be overlooked and every detail will imprint itself on our memory. Thus we will have first sharpened our powers of observation through these exercises and, as the fruit of this accurate observation, we will improve our memory.

We should take special care to retain not only names and main features of what we wish to remember, but also to retain vivid images of all the details. If we cannot remember some detail, we must try in the meantime to fill in the picture and make it a whole. We will then notice that our memory, in a kind of round-about way, gradually becomes reliable. Thus we can see how definite direction can be given for making thinking increasingly more practical.

There is still something else that is of particular importance. In thinking about some matters we feel it necessary to come to a conclusion. We consider how this or that should be done and then make up our minds in a certain way. This inclination, although natural, does not lead to practical thinking. All overly hasty thinking does not advance us but sets us back. Patience in these things is absolutely essential.

Suppose, for instance, we desire to carry out some particular plan. There are usually several ways that this might be done. Now we should have the patience first to imagine how things would work out if we were to execute our plan in one way and then we should consider what the results would be of doing it in another. Surely there will always be reasons for preferring one method over another, but we should refrain from forming an immediate decision. Instead, we should attempt to imagine the two possibilities and then say to ourselves: "That will do for now; I will now stop thinking about this matter." No doubt, some people will become fidgety at this point, and although it is difficult to overcome such a condition, it is extremely useful to do so. It now becomes possible to imagine how the matter might be handled in two ways and to decide to stop thinking about it for a while.

Whenever it is possible, action should be deferred until the next day, and the two possibilities considered again at that time. You will find that in the interim conditions have changed and that the next day you will be able to form a different, or at least a more thorough decision than could have been reached the day before. An inner necessity is hidden in things, and if we do not act with arbitrary impatience but allow this inner necessity to work in us (and it will), we will find the next day that it has enriched our thinking, making a wiser decision possible. This is extremely valuable.

We might, for example, be asked to give our advice on a problem and to make a decision. But let us not thrust forward our decision immediately. We should have the patience to place the various possibilities before ourselves without forming any definite conclusions, and we then should quietly let these possibilities work themselves out within us. Even the popular proverb says that one should sleep over a matter before making a decision.

To sleep over it is not enough, however. It is necessary to consider two or, better still, several possibilities that will continue to work within us when our "I" is not consciously occupied with them. Later on, when we return again to the matter in question, it will be found that certain thought forces have been stirred up within us in this manner, and that as a result our thinking has become more factual and practical.

It is certain that what people are looking for can always be found in the world, whether they are standing at a carpenter's bench, following a plough, or are a member of a profession. If they practice these exercises, they will become practical thinkers in the most ordinary matters of everyday life. If they train themselves in this way, they will view and approach things of the world in a way very different from before. Although at first these exercises may seem related only to one's own innermost life, they are entirely applicable and of the greatest importance precisely for the outer world. They have powerful consequences.

An example will demonstrate how necessary it is to think about things in a really practical way.

Imagine that a man climbs a tree for one reason or another. He falls from the tree, hits the ground, and is picked up dead. Now, the thought most likely to occur to us is that the fall killed him. We would be inclined to say that the fall was the cause, and death the effect. In this instance, cause and effect seem logically connected. However, this assumption may completely confuse the true sequence of facts, since the man may have fallen as the result of heart failure. To the observer, the outer event is exactly the same in both cases. Only when the true causes are known can a correct judgment be formed. In this case, the man may have already been dead before he fell, and the fall had nothing to do with his death. It is thus possible to invert cause and effect completely. In this instance, the error is clear, but often they are not so easily discernible. The frequency with which such errors in thinking occur is amazing. Indeed, it must be said that, in the field of science, conclusions are reached every day in which such confusion of cause and effect is permitted. Most people do not grasp this fact, however, because they are not familiar with the possibilities of thinking.

Still another example will show you clearly how such errors in thinking arise and how a person who has been practicing exercises like these can no longer make such mistakes. Suppose someone concludes that human beings today are descended from the ape. This means that what that person has come to know in the ape—the forces active in this animal—have attained higher perfection, and a human being is the result.

Now, to show the meaning of this theory in terms of thought, let's imagine that this person is the only human being on Earth, and that only the apes are present that, according to this theory, can evolve into human beings. The person now studies those apes with the greatest accuracy, right down to the smallest detail, and forms a concept of what lives in them. Excluding one's self and having never seen another human being, let the person now try to develop the concept of a human solely from a concept of the ape. This will be found to be impossible. The concept "ape" will never transform into the concept "human being."

If correct habits of thinking had been cultivated, this person would have thought, "My concept of the ape does not change into the concept of human. What I perceive in the ape, therefore, can never become a human being; otherwise my concept would have to change likewise. There must be something else present that I am unable to perceive." One would thus have to imagine an invisible, suprasensory entity behind the physical ape that the person would be unable to perceive—something that would alone make the ape's transformation into a human being a possible concept.

We will not discuss the impossibility of this case, but simply point out the erroneous thinking behind the theory. Through correct thinking, this person would have seen the impossibility of conceiving such a theory without assuming the existence of something suprasensory. Upon further investigation, you will discover that an overwhelmingly large number of people have committed this error of thinking. Errors such as these, however, no longer occur to those who have trained their thinking as suggested here.

Much of modern literature (especially that of the sciences) becomes a source of unpleasant experience for anyone capable of thinking correctly. The distorted and misguided thinking expressed in it can cause even physical pain in a person who has to work through it. It should be understood, however, that this is not said with any intent to slight the wealth of observation and discovery that has been accumulated by modern natural science and its objective methods of research.

Now let us consider "shortsighted" thinking. Most people are unconscious of the fact that their thinking is not factual, but that it is for the most part only the result of thought habits. The decisions and conclusions, therefore, of those whose thought penetrates the world and life will differ greatly from those belonging to people whose ability to think is limited or nonexistent. Consider the case of materialistic thinkers. To convince such people through reasoning—no matter how logical, sound, and good—is not easy. It is usually a useless exercise to try to convince those with little knowledge of life through reason. Such people do not see the reasons that make one or another statement valid and possible so long as the habit remains of seeing only matter in everything and simply adhering to this habit of thinking.

Today it can generally be said that people are not prompted by reasons when making statements but rather by the thinking habits behind these reasons. They have acquired habits of thought that influence all their feelings and sensations, and when reasons are put forth, they are simply the mask of the habitual thinking that screens these feelings and sensations. Not only is the wish often the father of the thought, but it can also be said that all our feelings and mental habits are the parents of our thoughts. Someone who knows life also knows how difficult it is to convince another person by means of logical reasoning. What really decides and convinces lies much deeper in the human soul.

There are good reasons for the existence of the anthroposophic movement and for the activities in its various branches. Everyone participating in the work of the Movement for any length of time comes to notice that they have acquired a new way of thinking and feeling. For the work in the various branches is not merely confined to finding logical reasons for things. A new and more comprehensive quality of feeling and sensation is also developed.

How some people scoffed a few years ago when they heard their first lectures in Spiritual Science. Yet today how many things have become self-evident to these same people who previously looked upon these things as impossible absurdities. In working in the anthroposophic movement one not only learns to modify one's thinking but one also learns to develop a wider perspective of soul life.

We must understand that our thoughts derive their coloring from far greater depths than are generally imagined. It is our feelings that frequently impel us to hold certain opinions. The logical reasons that are put forward are often a mere screen or mask for our deeper feelings and habits of thinking.

To bring ourselves to a point at which logical reasons themselves possess a real significance for us, we must have learned to love logic itself. Only when we have learned to love factuality and objectivity will logical reason be decisive for us. We should gradually learn to think objectively, not allowing ourselves to be swayed by our preference for this or that thought. Only then will our vision broaden in the sense that we do not merely follow the mental ruts of others but in such a way that the reality of the things themselves will teach us to think correctly.

True practicality is born of objective thinking—that is, thinking that flows into us from the things themselves. It is only by practicing such exercises as have just been described that we learn to take our thoughts from things. To do these exercises properly we should choose to work with sound and wholesome subjects that are least affected by our culture. These are the objects of nature.

To train our thinking using the things of nature as objects to think about will make really practical thinkers of us. Once we have trained ourselves in the practical use of this fundamental principle, our thinking, we shall be able to handle the most everyday occupations in a practical way. By training the human soul in this way a practical viewpoint is developed in our thinking.

The fruit of the anthroposophic movement must be to place really practical thinkers in life. What we have come to believe is not of as much importance as the fact that we should become capable of surveying with understanding the things around us. That Spiritual Science should penetrate our souls, thereby stimulating us to inner soul activity and expanding our vision, is of far more importance than merely theorizing about what extends beyond the things of the senses into the spiritual. In this, Anthroposophy is truly practical.

PART II

THE FUNDAMENTAL PRACTICE
OF ANTHROPOSOPHY

ANTHROPOSOPHY: AN OVERVIEW

INTRODUCTION

As mentioned before, the foundational books were written by Rudolf Steiner during the early years of his work, beginning in 1894 with *Intuitive Thinking as a Spiritual Path* (his "philosophy of freedom") and, in 1909, *An Outline of Esoteric Science*. At the very end of his life, he decided to write a series of short, aphoristic "leading thoughts" that summarize the whole of his worldview, Anthroposophy. These short contributions are like seeds—condensed kernels of wisdom that speak of much larger realities. One can take any single paragraph and use it as meditative content.

During my 2012 spring semester sabbatical from Antioch University, I spent concentrated time rereading Steiner's *Anthroposophical Leading Thoughts*. After some inner wrestling, I then took on the task of expressing each one in my own words. I did this partly to better understand, and partly to give modern expression to some of the gems Rudolf Steiner gave us almost a hundred years ago. In some cases I combined a few sentences, left out what appeared to be an awkward translation, or found a way to tie several thoughts together in a single expression. The reader should know that this was not an attempt at translation, but rather a free rendering by the author for the purposes of study. I recommend the exercise to others and certainly hope that future attempts may be different and stimulating. The purpose is to promote inner engagement and contemplation, without which the content has little purpose.

I decided to include the results of this sabbatical project as it serves as an interesting complement to the first part of the book. One could say that the foundational books form a solid basis upon which the whole edifice of Anthroposophy is built. The leading thoughts in this final section represent the fruit, the harvest of Rudolf Steiner's extraordinarily productive life. As such, the two parts of this book are like bookends to Anthroposophy. I hope the reader finds inspiration in both.

ANTHROPOSOPHY AS A PATH OF KNOWLEDGE

Sometimes, we have questions that cannot be answered by conventional means, such as the news media or the internet. There are situations when a person can feel an inner stirring—a longing for real answers that go beyond ordinary, informational knowledge. Sometimes this search can intensify and become burning questions about human nature, the origin of the universe, or the basis of healthy relationships. When this occurs, Anthroposophy can provide a sound path of knowledge that connects the spiritual in the seeker with the spiritual in the universe, the individual with the multidimensional.

In everyday life, science is founded on sensory perceptions and intellectual reasoning. But this can lead to a barrier in the path of inquiry, a limit where the soul of the seeker can die if not nourished with deeper meaning. Rather than stopping short at the limits of conventional knowledge, the human soul can become an opening for further exploration.

There are of course some who believe that knowledge derived just from sensory perception contains all that is worth knowing. Yet even in the act of thinking about these limits and this supposedly finite body of informational knowledge, human consciousness uses faculties that transcend these supposed limits. Eventually, many recognize that reflection (even reflection on our limitations) and the act of thinking demonstrate inner resources that can go beyond ordinary knowledge.

Our True Self

To develop emotional maturity and be successful in doing things on this Earth, the human being needs expansive knowledge. No matter how grand and beautiful nature may be, the natural world does not in itself give sufficient answers to the essential nature of the human being. During life, each human being holds together the materials and forces of the natural world in our physical body, but after death, nature receives that form and can no longer hold it together. The human form is dissolved and dispersed. Wisdom-filled nature can answer many question as to illness and dissolution of the physical body, but cannot fully explain how the human body is held together during life. How is the body maintained and held together during life? The presence of this question, when actively considered, awakens movement in the human soul and a longing for more expansive, spiritual paths for discovering the true nature of the Self.

Self-knowledge, found in this way, can bring inner peace. A person can find new inner dimensions of the soul as expressed in faculties such as thinking, feeling, and willing. Of course, the soul is influenced also by physical health and sickness, or the strengthening or weakening of the body. In sleep, many of these soul faculties are submerged below the threshold of consciousness. During life, human begins are naturally dependant on bodily conditions. The danger is that in this realm of ordinary existence, self-knowledge may be lost, or the search for it seen as a vain quest. Can there be self-knowledge that transcends the ordinary experiences of life? Can we have any certainty at all as to the true Self? Anthroposophy strives to answer this question on the basis of spiritual experience, not through opinion or belief, but on conscious experiences achieved through spirit research. Once achieved, this self-knowledge can become every bit as certain as the everyday experiences of the body.

A World of Living Connections

Astute perception reveals a difference between the inert, lifeless physical substances and those that abound in life and growth. One can respect the laws of nature that prevail on the Earth and rule all lifeless things. But when we start to contemplate the living world of plants, for instance, we soon realize that there are influences that come from the far distances of space—Sun, Moon, and other cosmic forces that free plants from mere earthly connections and promote life. Even the smallest plants are freed, so to speak, by the effects of light and warmth. The Earth and the cosmos are intimately connected.

In this setting, we find human beings placed on Earth with a transcendent being of soul and spirit. Human beings are connected to the earthly, lifeless world through a physical body, but through our life (etheric) body, we are connected to the wider expanse of the cosmos. Understanding this dual residency is crucial to gaining further insights into the activity of both the universe and human beings.

Consciousness

Thus far, our considerations of the human being have concerned the physical and etheric body, both of which reside in the unconscious. Of themselves, they do not lead to consciousness. In order for consciousness to light up in animals and humans something else must become active which is not the same as the physical or etheric. Precisely when the latter are relatively inactive, a third aspect of human nature comes to the fore—that is, the astral body.

The reality of this astral body can be discovered when we are stimulated from without or within to engage in thinking or reflecting. Through the strengthening of the soul by active thinking one can gradually develop inner organs of perception and the dawning of consciousness.

The physical and etheric aspects of human nature need to be held in check to make room for the work of consciousness. They furnish the ground, the support upon which consciousness can flourish, just as we all need the earth upon which to walk. The health of body and soul is vital to support the work of the spirit in human beings. Yet just as the planets in space do not require ground beneath them to orbit, so also the Spirit, when it looks not through the senses into matter but through its own power into spirit realms, needs no material foundation to call its conscious activity to life.

The Human "I," or Essential Self

Consciousness arises when the forces that hold together the physical and etheric bodies begin to disintegrate, thus making a pathway for the spirit to enter the human being. Yet if the disintegration process were to go too far, the organism would be destroyed. A process of reconstruction needs to occur, therefore, and self-awareness arises in rebuilding, or reassembling, these forces. Consciousness leads, therefore, to self-awareness when one creates, out of oneself, an after-image of an experience in ordinary consciousness. An image or picture is produced in the emptiness caused by the disintegration, and it passes into self-awareness when the emptiness has been filled up again from within. The being that does this filling, finding fulfillment, is experienced as the "I."

The "I" becomes a reality when the inner vision (the astral body) is taken a step further: rather than doing meditation as an act of passive devotion, one can activate thinking by having it permeated by will. When thinking is strengthened by the will, one can begin to perceive one's own "I."

Besides ordinary experiences of Self, there are three additional possible manifestations of the forms of the "I":

1. When consciousness takes hold of the etheric body, the "I" appears in active picture form, giving humans form, growth, and formative forces that help create and sustain the physical body
2. When consciousness takes hold of the astral body, the "I" is manifested as a member of the spiritual world from which it receives its forces
3. When consciousness works further, the "I" reveals itself as a self-contained spiritual being with a considerable amount of independence from the surrounding spiritual world.

Throughout the history of philosophy, people have sought for clarity as to the essential Self, or "I." In the description provided above, the "I" at first appears as a picture or as an image one might see on a movie screen. Then gradually one begins to experience the creative forces of the picture; one could say it starts to move, shape, and form. Then out of these shadowy reflections one can eventually sense the spiritual beings that sustain the creative forces, that nourish them. In this way, one can approach the transcendent "I."

Sleep, Dreams, Waking

One can say that the human being stands in three worlds: the "lower world" of physical, bodily development; a "middle world" of soul-nature that is highly personal; and an "upper world" that includes one's faculties of spirit striving. Human beings are indebted to nature for their bodily development and to the divine world for the gifts of the spirit, but as to the life of soul, that is our own portion.

There is spirit in every living thing in nature, but the spirit in nature is asleep. Just as the the "I" must be asleep at times to be more awake at other times, so the cosmic-spirit needs to sleep in nature to be more awake elsewhere.

In ordinary life, the human soul is like a dreamer. The spirit awakens the dreams of the soul so that it can participate in the world where its true being originates. The dreaming soul of human beings would lose its connection to the greater expanse of the universe if it did not occasionally heed the awakening call of spirit.

Denial of the Spirit

Failure to recognize the role of the spirit working in the inner life of human beings is the greatest hindrance to gaining insight into the spiritual world. Before the human soul can develop in a healthy way, people must become fully conscious of the active spiritual resources within their own being.

There are many today who cling to a mechanistic scientific worldview that physical causality is paramount, and all else is illusion. Those who hold this bias claim to base their views on observation and experiment, whereas they actually fail to observe fully the most crucial aspect of all—the whole human being. We have only to practice basic self-observation to see the activity of creative forces that cannot be explained through physical processes (love, artistic creation, innovation, etc.). Many mechanistic scientists thus try to divert attention from human beings or diminish their role to mere cogs in the wheel of nature.

True self-observation is thus the starting point for observing spirit at work. Just as the human body suffers when denied nourishment, human beings become stunted if not cognizant of the activity of the creative forces emanating from the spiritual world.

Death

At the time when human beings cross the threshold of death, all the impressions and the entire content of soul received during life through the senses begins to slip away. Instead, one's consciousness embraces a grand picture tableau of the whole of one's past life, even the things that may have gone unnoticed in everyday life but made an impression on the soul. After a few days these grand pictures begin to fade until a point at which the etheric body is laid aside, since it was the etheric that bore those images.

The astral body remains connected to the being of the deceased and now brings to consciousness all that lived in that person during sleep and while unconscious. Included in this content are the judgments instilled in the astral body by spirit beings during life— judgments concealed from consciousness during earthly life. As time passes after death, human beings live through their earthly life a second time, but now the content of the soul includes judgments of thought and action from a spiritual viewpoint. These are experienced in reverse order. This period of reliving the judgments of a past life last as long as the total time one spent asleep on Earth.

After this time has passed, the astral body is finally laid aside; the judgment of one's life is over, and one enters the spiritual world. Now we have new relationships—this time to purely spiritual beings, just as we were related to plants, animals, and humans on Earth. In our spiritual existence all that was once part of our outer world becomes part of our inner world, but now it is no longer only a perception, but also an experience. From the vantage point of the spirit worlds, we gaze out and see humanity as we previously saw the stars, clouds, mountains, and rivers.

Now forces are gathered within the human being that begin to work toward the future fashioning of another life on Earth.

Imagination, Inspiration, Intuition

Just as the physical body replenishes itself continuously thanks to our metabolism, so our inner nature unfolds and develops continuously between birth and death. As humans we live not only in space but also in time. During our life on Earth the soul and spirit show themselves outwardly in the development of the physical body. One catch glimpses of this inner, formative force in our imaginative life, an intermediary between the soul and the physical human being.

When we have inspirations we experience pictures of what we lived through when in a spiritual environment during the last journey between death and a new birth. Freed of physical constraints, we then experience our own true nature in relation to cosmic worlds.

Through intuitive knowledge we become conscious of what has lived on from prior earthly lives. Divested of a former connection to the physical world, this essence of being acts as a kind of spiritual kernel in our present life. This spirit essence can become an object of knowledge, which in turn encourages further development of imagination and inspiration.

Human Beings as a Picture of the Spiritual Worlds as Revealed in Head, Heart, and Hands

The fourfold aspects of the human being (physical, etheric, astral, and "I") develop in ways different from human activity. In the head, we see most strongly the signature of individuality. The "I," with the help of the astral or human consciousness, has helped shape the unique features found with each human head. Consideration of the human head shows that the astral and "I" exist somewhat separately from, or at least parallel with, the etheric and physical.

In contrast, the four human members are intimately interwoven in the limbs and metabolic part of the human being. The "I"-organization and astral body work within the physical and etheric organizations to vitalize and help growth and movement. The limbs are thus in constant development, as a germinating seed striving to become more permanent, like the head during a life on Earth.

Finally, the rhythmic aspect of the human being stands in the midpoint of these dynamics. Here the "I"-organization and the astral body alternate between uniting and loosening themselves again from the physical and etheric. The breathing and circulation, the movement of air and blood, are visible manifestations of this alternation between unifying and loosening. Inhaling makes the union visible, while exhaling exemplifies the loosening. Likewise the arterial blood is connected with unifying, and the venous blood is part of the loosening process.

In many ways the physical human body is a picture of the soul and spirit, and the working of invisible forces makes it intelligible. The head is the most complete and perfect symbolic picture of the soul and spirit, whereas the limbs are like a picture that is still unfinished and needs further work. The rhythmic system is in between these two opposites, and intermediary between head and limbs.

In the forms of the head, Imaginative pictures are coagulated, condensed to the point of physical density.

In trying to understand the rhythmic part of the human organism it is helpful to understand Inspirations. However, in penetrating the meaning of the limbs/metabolic system, we understand its functions best when one takes up the suprasensory aspect of Intuition.

Head — Imagination
Heart — Inspiration
Limbs — Intuition

Will

When one regards human beings as pictures of the spiritual world, then we can see higher, moral laws at work in the soul. For what we know as morality on the Earth is in itself a revelation of higher spiritual realities—they are connected, united.

In order to get things done on the Earth, human beings need motivation, directed energy, will. In the activity of the sense organs the will is not yet able to unfold fully, but in the rhythmic system it can work to some extent. This limited manifestation in the rhythmic system is due to the fact that in this realm, as with breathing, there is a constant coming-into-being and then passing away, which means the will is not yet free.

However, in the limbs and metabolic system, we have an arena where the will can become fully active. Here the will can work directly in everyday life. Thus we are able to accomplish things while on the Earth.

Destiny

Understanding of the will is a doorway toward perceiving the role of destiny. The clues for this cannot be found in the course of a single earthly life. Only when a human being has passed through the gate of death into the realm of the spirit can the spiritual nature of the will come into full effect. In the journey after death, we become in our essential being an image of what we did during our earthly lives—we begin to form our next earthly life. Destiny is prepared in the spiritual worlds, and this impulse is then willed into the next incarnation on Earth.

When exploring destiny it is helpful to take examples from historical figures, men and women whose lives have been influenced in ways that cannot be fully explained by the usual study of biography. One can, for example, find an event that occurred in youth that shaped events later in a person's life. One can also find examples in which something good inexplicably turns negative, or a misfortune turns out well in the end. Real biographical events are much more helpful than a string of theories. Gradually one learns to "read" how events of destiny can come into a person's life in such a way that the causes cannot be found in present biographical circumstances. The study of destiny already points the investigator in the direction of former lives on Earth.

It is wrong to think that the unconscious must always remain in the realm of the unknown. In learning to look at life through the lens of destiny, we can bit by bit lift elements of the unconscious into everyday consciousness. As this occurs, one realizes that things arising from destiny often have their origin prior to this life on Earth. One begins to look beyond outer nature, beyond ordinary consciousness, to a realm of spiritual origins.

From an intense study of biography we begin to apprehend destiny, and from the study of destiny we start to look at the development of repeated Earth lives. Human souls, passing from epoch to epoch in repeated lives on Earth, carry the results of one historic age into another. History becomes more real and abundant as we see the intermingling of human striving and interactions over repeated lives. Likewise, we can gaze more deeply into any individual human soul by tracing the historic origins. Thus, we arrive at a study of karma.

Karma

As has been already mentioned, the journey after death takes place in stages. In the first few days after death the whole of the past earthly life is seen in pictures. This is a process of letting go so that the soul-spirit can move on. After about a third of the past earthly life has been reviewed in a second phase, the soul experiences the ethical effects of deeds done in the last life. Only then does one enter a purely spiritual epoch of existence, which lasts a long time. Along with other human souls with whom we have been connected, and with spiritual beings of the hierarchies, we start to fashion our next life on Earth with the direction given by karma.

Spiritual research is needed in order to fathom the riddles of karma, but anyone can understand the results of this research if one uses common intelligence and an open mind.

During life the human being belongs to the three kingdoms of mineral, plant, and animal, but the journey after death shows that humans also belong to the spirit kingdom. We experience the mineral kingdom in the forms all around us, and the growing plant kingdom shows us life forces, or the etheric. The astral body helps us become aware of impulses and sensations, as is the case with the animal kingdom. However, the crowning of human existence is the self-conscious spiritual life that connects humans with the cosmos.

Thinking, Feeling, Willing

Our ordinary, everyday thoughts are mere reflected images. The reason we feel alive in our thoughts is because we experience ourselves as living in them. This vitality has its source in spirit beings (third hierarchy) who work through our thinking.

In regard to our feelings, the immediate experience is often that they arise out of the body, such as in pleasure or pain. In fact, our bodily experiences connect us to the world of nature. Yet once again, if one delves deeper, one finds that feelings also have an independent character that is supported by spirit beings (second hierarchy).

When we engage in deeds of will, our attention is not focused on ourselves but on the outer world. When we walk, we do not focus on our feet but rather our goal. In willing we forget our body, because will does not belong to our own nature but rather to the spirit kingdom (first hierarchy).

In perceiving the world through our senses we can see only the surface, a portion of that which lies beneath. One needs penetrative spiritual observation to uncover the living realities of the deeds of human beings in past ages in time. One delves deeply enough to encounter destiny; one finds not only new ways of understanding the external world, but also the human "I," for this self is not only self-contained but also part of an expansive world.

In thinking we have the possibility of freedom. In feeling, the world soul is ever creative. In our willing we experience spiritual creation beyond humanity, beyond one person, as a part of the wide universe.

Human Beings Are More than Just a Physical Body

As mentioned earlier, through our physical body we can relate to the natural world around us, but through our higher members we can connect with the spiritual kingdoms. For example, in the etheric body the intelligence of the cosmos becomes embodied in the human being. Specifically, this cosmic intelligence helps to shape the etheric body just as physical forces shape the physical. We are shaped by cosmic wisdom.

Through the astral body the spiritual world implants moral impulses into the human being (often portrayed in classic fairy tales). These moral forces are not only thoughts, but active spiritual beings that help shape the human organism.

Thanks to our "I"-organization, we are able to experience ourselves—even in the physical body—as spirit. This is possible due to the activity of spiritual beings who themselves live in the physical world.

Hierarchies

Language used in Anthroposophy for such aspects as the hierarchies (below) can seem confusing or difficult. However, for every spiritual reality there is also a practical manifestation that can be grasped with sound common sense. For instance:

First Hierarchy: *Seraphim, Cherubim, Thrones.* These spiritual beings reveal themselves in forms that manifest in the world of the senses, in sense-perceptible imagery. We can experience the majesty of those beings at work in the sunset or sunrise, the mist rising from a lake, the rolling waves on the seashore. These are the acts or creations of spiritual beings, now manifest through nature.

Second Hierarchy: *Kyriotetes, Dynamis, Exusiai.* These spiritual beings reveal themselves not in sense-perceptible forms, but in purely spiritual imagery. We could look to the content of dreams or the inner picture of someone who has crossed the threshold.

Third Hierarchy: *Archai, Archangeloi, Angeloi.* These spiritual beings reveal themselves not in sense-perceptible forms or in spiritual imagery, but in the life of the soul—specifically in how thinking, feeling, and willing are expressed in the human soul. When we think, feel, or act, we are working with the beings of the third hierarchy, and they are working through us.

All the hierarchies work together on the kingdoms of nature and human beings on Earth. We can see an outer manifestation of their collective action in the starry heavens at night. Star wisdom is spirit knowledge seen from afar.

Waking, Dreaming, Sleeping

Thanks to our waking consciousness, we experience ourselves as contemporary people on the world stage. Nevertheless, the price we pay is that our waking awareness conceals from us the fact that the third hierarchy is present in all our experiences. We think, feel, and act in daily life but are often unaware of what is working through these soul forces. We cannot see the direct effects of the journey between death and rebirth.

When we dream, we often have chaotic experiences that result from a lack of harmony with the spirit beings around us. But when we work through to a state of Imaginative consciousness we gradually realize that the other pole of dreams is the work of the second hierarchy in our transitory states of consciousness. We can then begin to see how, between death and rebirth, the spirit world helps to build up our inner being.

In dreamless sleep we unconsciously experience our unity with the spirit being of the world. When we work through to a state of Inspired consciousness we can become aware that the first hierarchy is present in these sleep experiences. We experience unconsciously the effects of past earthly lives, and then with the help of Intuitive consciousness we can develop a clear vision of karma and how the past influences our destined course of life in the present.

Karma

Just as our senses help us to see the outer world around us, likewise we need to observe our thinking to become aware of our will impulses. This is important because it is through will impulses that we have a doorway to former lives on Earth.

Ordinarily, with ideas transmitted through the senses, we live in the physical world around us. For us to function on a daily basis, karma must be silent in our thinking. One could say that in forming everyday ideas, we forget our karma. However, in the manifestations of the will, karma works itself out. However, this activity remains unconscious. Only by lifting to conscious Imagination what is otherwise unconscious in the will can we apprehend karma. Human beings then feel their destiny within them.

However, when inspiration and Intuition enter the Imagination, then besides the impulses of the present, the outcome of former earthly lives becomes perceptible in the working of the will. Then past lives are revealed, working themselves out in the present.

One could say that thinking, feeling, and willing live in the soul of human beings. But within thinking, there is always a bit of feeling and willing, within feeling a bit of willing and thinking, and within willing there is also a small portion of feeling and thinking.

It is in the feeling and willing of the life of thought that we find the karmic consequences of past lives on Earth. The thinking and willing contained in the life of feeling karmically helps determine human character. The thinking and feeling in the life of will seek to tear the present earthly life away from its karmic connections.

In the feeling and willing in thinking, human beings live out karma of the past. In the thinking and feeling of willing, we prepare our karma for the future.

Thinking

Thoughts reside not in the brain, but rather have their true seat in the etheric, in the life forces of the human being. Thoughts are forces of real life and being. They imprint themselves on the physical body, just as our footprints are visible in the snow. These imprinted thoughts, however, are not the real thing; they have only the shadowy character that moves in our everyday consciousness.

The small amount of feeling that lives in our thoughts comes from the astral body, and the portion of willing comes from the "I." When sleeping, the human etheric body is infiltrated by our thoughts. But a sleeping person does not know it because during sleep the astral and "I," the feeling and willing elements, have withdrawn. They return when we awake.

During sleep, the astral and "I" lose their connection with the "thoughts" of the etheric body, and this allows them to connect with karma, beholding events arising from repeated earthly lives. We can experience the reality of this through suprasensory consciousness.

Over time, human thought has descended from a living experience of the suprasensory to the world of senses. We used to experience thoughts with our whole being: "I"-being and the astral, etheric, and physical bodies. Then over time thoughts descended through these members until today when they have rooted themselves in the physical. As a result, the living experience of thinking first became mere images, then fleeting inner stirring as an echo of the soul, until finally thoughts are often only dead shadows of the spiritual. But along the way, the will has come to life in new ways; Archangel Michael can lead us back again through thinking to direct experience of the spiritual worlds.

Michael is now helping humankind return upward along the path traveled, leading the will upward, retracing the former descent into abstract Intelligence. Michael shows the way so that humans can follow in freedom. This is what distinguishes the journey from previous epochs. In the past, the hierarchies not only revealed their working but also used human development to evolve themselves. Thus, human beings could not be free. Now the situation is different: with the help of Michael human beings an find their way back to a direct connection with the spiritual worlds with heart and soul, but this time as self-directed, free beings.

Freedom is given to all human beings who find themselves at our present stage of human evolution. Freedom is now the essential element of consciousness. The mission of Michael is intimately connected to this coming into being of freedom today.

Competition for the Human Soul: Lucifer and Ahriman

Today human beings mostly see the accomplished work, the outer forms of nature and the material world around us. Few see a connection to the divine anymore. At most, we tend to see the image of reality in ideas, but not the true sources. When we become fixated in the things of this world, we can fall into the grip of Ahriman, a spiritual being that tries to tie us to the Earth. However, Michael can help us find a right relationship to nature that is not dominated by the hardening forces of Ahriman.

Looking back into past ages can be falsified by Lucifer, and thinking into the future can be deceived by the allurements of Ahriman. The being of Michael helps us guard against both tendencies.

Freedom

Our actions are free when natural processes, whether within us or from without, can play an active role. In fact, when an individual works freely, a natural process is suppressed in that person. When we are unfree in our action, we are ruled by natural processes; such actions have a predestined character. When we unite ourselves with Michael, we can take hold of life in freedom.

Cosmic thoughts are not just ideas, but represent the activity of beings. The cosmic thoughts that carry humankind into the future come from Michael. We need to get away from the concept of an undefined spirituality and vague sentiment. Instead, we need to form definite, clear ideas about the spiritual world.

Today we live in the age of the consciousness soul, a time of independent intellectuality, of direct connection between sense-free thinking and the spiritual worlds.

Previously, Luciferic activity tried to prevent humankind from understanding and from entering direct connection with physical existence. Lucifer tried to hold humankind back in the forces of cosmic childhood. Michael now is at work to help humankind preserve independent thinking.

Human Loss

In this age human beings have tried with limited success to use the intellect to connect with faith and ritual. These attempts have brought uncertainty and doubt into the human soul. Rather than experiencing faith as a direct experience, humans have tried to use logic to explore spiritual realities. They have tried to use logical deduction to understand the contents of sacred ritual. This path of inquiry will not work, as these matters today need to employ spiritual Imaginations to reestablish true connections to the sacred.

Although Michael cannot have direct contact with the present earthly world, he can work through human intelligence. This has the effect of a kind of disturbance in the cosmic balance of things, and human beings are forced to fall back upon themselves as they negotiate the path from soul-less logic to new imaginative perceptions.

Michael's mission has been facilitated by certain key individuals, Rosicrucians, who arranged their outward life on Earth so that their daily actions would not interfere with their inner life of soul. They could develop inner forces that enabled them to work with Michael without entangling him in earthly events. This is an example of cosmic and earthly collaboration.

When human beings lost a living picture of their own being, they felt powerless. Wanting the ancient picture of humanity to arise again, people sought for meaning in natural science and history. But rather than finding fulfillment this way, this search for the true being of humanity lead only to apparent success, to illusions. All the while, with anxiety and suffering Michael witnessed how human beings avoided any real contemplation of the spirit; without this, they severed all previous links that had connected them with Michael.

The Ages of Time

As portrayed in the myth of Persephone, there is a rhythmic repetition of seasons in which we see a cycle of life and withdrawal. There is a phase of ensouling nature with eternal forces, just as Christ's descent ensouls humankind with the Logos. The evolution of human beings stands within a grand cosmic, rhythmic repetition, but the Mystery of Golgotha is a mighty, one-time event.

There are various time periods in human evolution: heavenly history, mythological history, and earthly history. In the earthly period we find the divine-spiritual working in free intelligence and will that no one can calculate. Yet we also find the calculable order of the world body that is opposed by Lucifer. Whereas Ahriman stands against all, Lucifer creates free intelligence and will in human beings.

The event of Golgotha is a cosmic deed, given freely. It sprung from universal love, and can only be understood by the love in human beings.

Looking back at the history of the human being, one can distinguish three stages:

1. Human beings did not exist as distinct individualities but were seeds in the divine spiritual. The cosmos consisted of spiritual beings and primal forces one could call Archai.
2. In an intermediate stage, human beings became individuals but were still attached through thinking and willing to the divine spiritual world. They did not have their present personality of detachment, but were still intricately bound up with spiritual processes. Here, human beings were in the domain of the Archangeloi, and owing to the influence of Lucifer and Ahriman, they descended more deeply into the physical than they would have without this intervention.

3. At this stage, human beings experience themselves in their human form and figure as detached from the divine-spiritual world. We stand face-to-face with the environment as individual personalities. In this period, humans are in the domain of the Angeloi, who wield their influence only in the astral body and "I." This stage began with the age of Atlantis.

Likewise, if we look at life between death and rebirth, we find distinct periods or stages. Along this journey between lives, we first live entirely within the hierarchy of the Archai, those who prepared the human form and figure in ages past. Then human beings experience the unfolding of free self-awareness, which was possible with a distinct human form. This process continues so that in the journey between death and rebirth the human being experiences how the microcosm grew out of the macrocosm.

Before human beings could attain self-awareness, the macrocosm had to go through a death process. However, thanks to the plants, minerals, and animals on Earth, new, life-kindling forces have begun to radiate out toward the cosmos. The past has thrown its shadows, but the future is now filled with the seed of a new reality. All these crosscurrents meet in the human being; both death and life. We participate in the germinating life as well as in the dead and dying of the old world. From the dead, we derive the forces of thought; from the germinating life, our forces of volition. The old had to die so that humankind could separate from the old world order and attain self-awareness. The newly attained thought forces make us free, and thanks to human will forces, the macrocosm is springing into life again.

Sleeping, Waking, Dreaming

To be fully awake, human beings need to lift themselves out of direct experience of reality in its true form in order to enter the shadowy realm of personal thinking. In this severed state, we can be self-conscious and free in our thinking.

In contrast, when we are asleep, we lose consciousness of self and live fully in the environment of the Earth.

Dreaming is a transition state of half-consciousness in which the potent world-existence weaves in and out of a state of partial consciousness. This potent world existence is the spirit source out of which humans built their physical bodies, and dies upon waking into the shadows of thought. However, in the process we gain our maturity as conscious humans.

Freedom and Thinking

When we have ideas, they often have a picture quality. Our abstract thoughts help us exercise freedom, in that we can disconnect from our environment and our past. These pictures do not compel, and when we share knowledge in picture form we can leave our listeners free as well.

In contrast, in our unconscious life we are still organically connected to our past lives, in a more intimate connection to a spiritual state of being. We are tied to our past experiences.

With the help of Michael's activity and the Christ impulse, we can leap across the above gulf and be free in relation to the cosmos; we can be free in our connection to the spiritual world.

This is possible also because in thinking, even though we live in the earthly realm, we do not become submerged in it with our full being. These days we are seeking communion of spirit and nature, of thinking and being. Thus our "I" finds fulfillment in these times.

One of the results of our immersion in the sense world is a kind of stupefaction in our thinking. In this state, we are susceptible to Ahrimanic powers that make us feel that the stupefying experience of sense impressions represents progress, such as in the latest gadget we must own but do not understand. We need to find the inner strength to fill our world of ideas with light in a way that they are independent of the sense world, and in their independence filled with light reawaken our kinship with the cosmos. This will provide a true foundation for the festivals of Michael.

In sensory perception and in thought we are not alone or isolated, but part of the contents of the world; we are world. Yet when we live in pure soul and spirit, accessible through Inspiration, we meet our own destiny. With our sensory system, we live in the physical body; with thinking, in the etheric; but when both are cast aside in living activity of knowledge, we find ourselves in the astral body. Then we experience self-knowledge.

Memory and Conscience

What radiates from the Divine Spiritual Being into the physical-etheric of human nature and lives in the force of sensory perception takes form in memory. By contrast, what comes from human beings' past lives is purely of soul and spirit and lives on in the astral body and "I." This stream of influence lives on in us as conscience.

The two impulses come together, from both sides, in the rhythmic human organization. In life and our experience of rhythm, memory is carried into willing and conscience is carried into the life of ideas.

Ancient Traditions

Human beings today in the age of science share a sorrowful perspective: as knowledge of the outer world grew by leaps and bounds, knowledge of the spiritual world receded to the point in which many feel it is no longer possible. Ancient traditions lived on in some quarters as a matter of tradition and faith. In this situation of uncertainty in the Middle Ages, two pathways seemed open to those seeking knowledge: Nominalism and Realism. The former represented unbelief in the spirit content of human ideas, whereas the latter embraced the reality of ideas, but it finds true fulfillment only in Anthroposophy.

The Greeks and Romans helped humanity unfold the intellectual or mind soul to a high degree of perfection. Then in the time of early Christianity until the birth of the spirit soul, people were able to "explain" the world of the spirit but no longer experience it directly in living consciousness. Then the people who migrated from the northeast toward Rome took hold of the mind soul and added to it an element of feeling. The inner life of these people was waiting for the present time when a reunion of the soul and spirit would once more be possible.

Technology and Science

Human beings today stand at a tipping point. Will we, as some have predicted, become just like a machine? Will the laws of industry and technology rule us, drawing us ever further down into subnature? Or will we be able to reclaim the spirit and find the inner strength to rise above technology, remain human in an age of gadgets? The theories we hold about nature and the human being will be of utmost importance in making sure humans remain in control of technology and can bring moral technique to bear on matters of atomic energy and other potentially destructive uses of the forces of nature. The human being is the fulcrum of this equation.

Appendix 1: The Six Exercises

1. Control of Thoughts

Empty the soul, and take up a simple thought, for example an everyday object like a pin. It is better to choose simple and uninteresting objects. Then say to yourself, "I will start from this thought, and by my own initiative I will connect with it methodically what can be connected with the object I have chosen." At the end of the exercise, the starting thought should stand before the mind as fresh as at the beginning. A different object may be chosen each day, or the same one used.

The aim of this exercise is to acquire control of what lives in one's soul as thought, and not be distracted by all kinds of fortuitous associations or memories that come unbidden into consciousness.

2. Control of Action (Will)

Choose a simple act not required by normal daily life, and carry it out each day. It is helpful to choose an act which can cover an extended period of time (for example the care of a plant that needs daily watering). But the task should be relatively insignificant, so that it must be carried out from one's own initiative, and one is not carried along by the interest of the task itself. After a time, add a second and a third task.

If possible, continue the first exercise as well, so that its fruits do not fade.

3. Equanimity in Feeling

Strive for equilibrium in pain and pleasure, sorrow and joy. Avoid extremes of mood—excessive rapture or excessive depression. This exercise consists essentially of recollecting a mood that should then pervade throughout daily life, and bring a mood of inner peace.

4. Positivity

Seek in all experiences of life the good, the ideal, the beautiful. Even within the ugly or depraved, something beautiful and good is hidden. This is an exercise for withholding criticism, for finding a standpoint, which can enter with love into a person or situation, and asks how they come to be like this, leading to a will to help rather than simply criticize.

5. Openness of mind and heart

Try to develop the habit of meeting every new experience without prejudice, with an open mind. Previous experiences and judgments must not obscure recognition of new truths.

6. Uniting all five exercises in rhythmic sequence

Try to practice each exercise in sequence (for example one each day, for a period of time). This gradually brings a strong harmonizing influence into the soul.

THE EIGHTFOLD PATH
AND THE SIX ACCESSORY EXERCISES

In describing the meditative life for the present day, Rudolf Steiner emphasized again and again the importance of two sets of exercises, which bring about a general ordering and strengthening of the life of the soul. One set—the "Eight Exercises"—is a modern version of the "Eightfold Path" outlined by the Gautama Buddha. These may be linked to the days of the week, as described below. The second set—the "Six Accessory Exercises"—should be practiced at the same time, for example one per month (though another rhythm may be adopted, as long as it is sustained regularly).

At the beginning, it is helpful to concentrate on one of the eight exercises for a longer period at first (e.g., for two weeks, and then, after working through the whole sequence once, working though it again with one week for each exercise, until ready to take one of the exercises each day).

The Eight exercises are really seven plus one; similarly the six are really five plus one. The way to practice the eight exercises is to think intensely about the quality indicated, forming in the mind as clear a conception as possible, and holding it for five minutes. After each exercise, the eighth exercise should be taken for a further five minutes. The description of each exercise given below is based on those given by Rudolf Steiner in a number of places.

The method of practicing the six exercises is implicit in the description of them. Here, too, five minutes a day should be spent on one of these exercises.

Given below is a brief description of the exercises, followed by a suggested "work plan" which may be found helpful for beginning this work.

The Eight Exercises

Saturday	Right Thinking
Sunday	Right Resolve
Monday	Right Speaking
Tuesday	Right Action
Wednesday	Right Way of Life
Thursday	Right Endeavor
Friday	Right Remembrance
Plus:	Right Meditation

Right Thinking (Saturday)

Admit only significant ideas and thoughts. Learn gradually to separate the important from the unimportant, the real from the unreal, the eternal from the ephemeral, the true from the false. Listen to what people say with inner quietness, refraining from approving or disapproving judgment and from criticism. In this way one arrives at the habit of forming opinions that are not influenced by sympathy or antipathy.

Right Resolve (Sunday)

Cultivate steadfastness. Make resolutions only after full consideration of even the most insignificant points. Avoid thoughtless acts and meaningless ones. For every act have sufficient reasons. Do no needless thing. When convinced of the rightness of a resolve, abide by it unfalteringly.

Right Speaking (Monday)

In speech with others, say only what has sense and meaning. Make your conversation thoughtful. Do not be afraid to be silent often. Try not to use too many or too few words. Never talk for the sake of talking, or merely to pass the time.

Right Action (Tuesday)

Make your actions as far as possible harmonious with your surroundings. Weigh all actions carefully so that the Eternal may speak through them, so that they may be good for the whole and for the lasting welfare of others.

Right Way of Life (Wednesday)

In the management of life, seek to live in conformity with both nature and spirit. Be not over-hasty nor idle. Look upon life as an opportunity for work and development, and live accordingly.

Right Endeavor (Thursday)

Do not attempt what is beyond your powers, but also omit nothing for which they seem adequate. Set before yourself ideals, which coincide with the highest ideals of a human being—for example, the aim of practicing such exercises as these in order to be able better to help and advise one's fellow human beings, if not immediately, then later in life. One can also say that this exercise consists in making all these exercises into a habit of life.

Right Remembrance (Friday)

Strive to learn as much as possible from life. All experiences have something to teach. When opportunity offers, we should handle a situation more wisely than previously. Experience is a rich treasure, and we should consult it before doing anything. Watch the actions of others and compare them with the ideal— lovingly, not critically. We can learn much from observing others, including children. Aim to remember all that you have learned in this way.

Right Meditation (To accompany each of the above)

Each day, at a set time if possible, turn inward and take stock, test your way of life, review your store of knowledge, ponder your duties, consider the aim and true purpose of life, and reflect on your own imperfections and mistakes. In short, distinguish what is significant and has lasting value while renewing your resolve to take up worthwhile tasks.

❦

These two sets of exercises neutralize, heal, and protect the soul from any harmful influences, which may come from other eso- teric exercises, so that only the positive results remain. They also make secure the positive results of exercises in concentration and meditation. A fundamental attitude to accompany all these exercises is that they belong to the rightful evolution of humankind. Students must try to banish all egoism from their practice.

A SUGGESTED WORK PLAN

Weeks 1–2	Right Thinking	Weeks 1–4	Control of
Weeks 3–4	Right Resolve		Thoughts
Weeks 5–6	Right Speaking	Weeks 5–8	Control of Action
Weeks 7–8	Right Action		
Weeks 9–10	Right Way of Life	Weeks 9–12	Equanimity in
Weeks 11–12	Right Endeavor		Feeling
Weeks 13–14	Right Remembrance	Weeks 13–16	Positivity
Week 15	Right Thinking		
Week 16	Right Resolve		
Week 17	Right Speaking	Weeks 17–20	Openness of
Week 18	Right Action		Mind and Heart
Week 19	Right Way of Life		
Week 20	Right Endeavor		
Week 21	Right Remembrance	Weeks 21–24	All five exercises
Week 22	One exercise each day,		in sequence, one
	beginning on a Saturday		each day
	with Right Thinking		

Continue for three weeks. The whole sequence may then be repeated for another six months if desired.*

❧

Those who have been traveling out over the country report hearing from all sides questions like this: "Can't we expect

---

* Compiled in this form by J. Davy, based mainly on suggestions given by Rudolf Steiner in *How to Know Higher Worlds* and *Guidance in Esoteric Training*.

our government to be honest and dependable any longer? Isn't democracy workable? When our economic system itself threatens to break down under the guidance of our expert thinkers and planners: What has gone wrong with us?"

We know that government is people. But, people collectively, not individually. When people join in common tasks the insights and inspirations of individuals tend to be compromised, so as to "get along," and this provides the soil for obstructing forces to take root and build up independent power for their own purposes. These are the super-human forces of hindrance built into the very structure of human existence in order to stimulate people's awareness, and resistance to them. By such struggles they develop their own capacities, on and on, toward "freedom," that basic urge in all humankind. We see it growing stronger all over the Earth, so evidently it is the way of self-development. But this requires becoming aware of what there is to be free from—power and glory, and all the other false diversions put in our path.

EXERCISE 1: CONCENTRATION

Make a mental picture of some simple object, for instance an ordinary pencil with an eraser on one end. Excluding every other thought, and feeling, ask yourself questions such as, "What is it made of? How is it put together?" etc., so as to keep the mind pinned to the one point of interest. Or take a simple phrase like, "Rain freshens the air." Keep watch for ideas trying to break in on your train of thought, such as, "I must remember to stop at the market today," or something else wholly unrelated. We are so accustomed to distractions and adjusting to interruptions. Five minutes on just one thing! Not so easy.

EXERCISE 2: CONTROLLING THE WILL

Choose some simple act you would not ordinarily do at the time of day you now determine, such as carrying a sofa-cushion to a chair in the next room—something without meaning or value but merely arbitrary. To do this requires releasing an impulse deep inside you that prods you to remember what you have chosen to do at the given time, then to DO IT. In this way you are learning to obey your own commands. The more trivial the action the more difficult it is to arouse the will to do it—without fail.

To halfheartedly desire something that seems impossible to attain creates dissatisfactions and instability in the soul. But applying a strengthened will to focus on the matter either shows it to be an idle longing, therefore to be dismissed, or the will takes hold and transforms what seemed impossible into the possible, and the desire is fulfilled. With what satisfaction then! As a result the soul itself is made stronger.

EXERCISE 3: EQUANIMITY

Here we try to avoid swinging between sympathy and antipathy toward what comes to us from outside. Instead we try to maintain a balance between the two extremes. By consciously paying attention to our reactions we come to see how letting ourselves be swayed from side to side prevents us from seeing the true nature of whatever meets us. We become more receptive to what lives in our environment if we avoid extreme expressions of, for instance, joy and sorrow; the one tending to carry us out of ourselves, the other plunging us deep into a depression. It is important that we keep an equable mood, so that no sudden situation leads to an outburst of anger, or catches us up in anxiety and fear.

Rudolf Steiner said, "The equilibrium we already *appear* to possess is less important than practicing what we lack. Though life may have taught us much in this respect, the abilities we gain by our own effort are what count."

EXERCISE 4: POSITIVITY

To cultivate this soul attribute does not mean to avoid all criticism; close our eyes to what is bad, false, inferior. It is not possible to find the bad to be *good* and the false *true*. It does mean to attain an attitude of sympathetically entering into any situation so as to see its best attributes. It means responding to what is praiseworthy, seeking out what is the good, constructive, beautiful, in *all* things and situations. This develops the power to nullify evil influences.

Maintaining a positive attitude itself sends forth constructive influences, and it does much to overcome the all too frequent lack of attentiveness to the subtle details in situations that are so revealing, and help one to know how to make them constructive.

To be positive does not mean to be aggressive, only to approach a person or situation in a spirit of constructive interest.

EXERCISE 5: OPEN-MINDEDNESS, IMPARTIALITY

By whatever regulating forces we have been living heretofore, and are used to—beliefs, customs, laws—we should keep ourselves ready at any moment to take in a new idea, a new experience, with total impartiality. Life is continually evolving, sometimes at a rapid pace, and we need to see what is for the good, and what is detrimental to it; also how we are to proceed in relating to it. New manifestations of truth must find us ready at any time to receive them. Our thinking and our impulses of will grow more mature as we freely take in, without bias, what is new.

While we do not disregard past ideas and experiences, we must be willing to experience continually what is new. We must have faith in the possible contradictions of the old by the new, as being the way of evolution.

Therefore, we implant in our consciousness the need never to fail in maintaining an impartial, open mind, free of prejudice.

❧

For the sixth practice period—and very important: When you have successfully completed these five exercises—making sure that if you missed one day on a given exercise you have gone back and started over again—begin now to practice them again but with more frequent interchange.

Here, it is only the individuals, units of society, who can be the watchdogs and can develop their inborn powers to be able to protect our collective activities from defeat and preserve civilization.

From earliest history people have been guided by higher forces in ways suited to the stage of their development. But what is right for us now in this twentieth century, which has been carried so deeply into materialistic doing and thinking? Again, leadership has come to give guidance, anticipating our needs for meeting the growing hazards of our age. It came at the turn of the century through one individual specially qualified to show the way: Rudolf Steiner, renowned for his cultural innovations in all fields of human activity. He ushered in a new era of knowledge beyond material limits, including details concerning the forces at work in the human soul and spirit, and what they require for healthy living. But to open minds and hearts of the present day to taking in freely such expanded knowledge needs some preparation; so he gave the following exercises to strengthen the soul for this new outstretching experience. If carried out with firm intent they likewise strengthen the soul for meeting the situations in daily life with clearer understanding and more security.

✺

How to do the exercises: Since their purpose is to gain control of the mind, of one's feelings, and impulses of the will-to-do, the first test comes already in requiring one to devote at least five minutes of practice each day, preferably at the same chosen time, for one week before taking up the next exercise. If a day is missed, one is to begin again to make sure of carrying through the seven-day stretch without a break. The second week then is devoted exclusively to the second exercise, and so on through the five weeks. Since it is *continuity of effort* that builds the power of control, more can be gained by extending the practice period to two, three, or even four weeks. This of course requires more discipline to maintain the longer stretch without a break, but such discipline brings far-reaching rewards. Gradually it develops in the soul firmness, certainty, equilibrium, and that consistency which makes for "character." Therefore, try *one month* on each exercise, if you can sustain it.

Do them in pairs—one pair each day for a week, another pair the next week, and so on for five weeks *without a break.*

You might do it so: #1 paired with #3, 2 with 4, and 1 with 5; then 2 with 3, and 4 with 5, or however you feel they are most needed.

The purpose of this interchanging practice is to bring about a good balance in the effectiveness of the exercises.

Presumably, during this time you will also be absorbing knowledge concerning the constitution of human beings and the world in which we live, so that what might seem to be the slow pace of the exercises doesn't strain your patience in "getting on with it."

"These exercises are suitable for anyone to do who is in earnest about it," said Rudolf Steiner. "The important point is not to aim for any special achievement—such as attaining 'spiritual vision,' 'enlightenment,' or the like—but to keep steadily going in the direction one has chosen, regardless of results. Whereas the usual attitude in our material world is to 'go get,' to accomplish, spiritual results come of themselves when we practice steadily. Spiritual qualities, their value, come to us, but only when we are ready to receive them—to bear them. The movement is reversed."

He also said, "When these exercises are conscientiously carried out it will be found that they yield, gradually, much more than at first appeared to be in them."

Appendix 2: Beyond Memories

Having described some of the essential characteristics of human beings in general, the next step is to look at some of the qualities that contribute to the individuality of each person. When it comes to working together in organizations, each person's contribution is very much affected by one's individual life path, accumulated experiences, memories, and yearnings. Rather than suppress these individual contributions, organic organizations weave them into the tapestry of the culture.

Looking at a family photo album will bring back memories, some humorous and some poignant, startling, or wistful. The photos spark other mental images, and soon one is reliving past experiences. When the album is finally closed, we are different. Our souls have expanded; our hearts are full. There is a breadth and depth that was not there before. It wasn't just the photos or the images of our children when they were younger, but something new has happened. In remembering, we are recreating past realities. Each of us is a changed person through our remembering.

If one has the courage to look within, one finds a treasure trove of memories that have collected in the soul. Gradually, some of our memories sank below the threshold of daily consciousness, and thus we may not be aware of all that rests there. Such experiences mature over time, and when we decide to draw them forth again, they rise above the threshold of consciousness in a new way. They have become personal resources. For example, I can see things more clearly because my vision has grown over time. This processing of experiences nourished the part of me that is *always* me—my spirit. Consequently, we are often drawn to older people for advice, because they have grown in spirit through the years. The spirit is nourished by the treasures of the past offered up by the soul.

Most people have a vague understanding of this. But let us take a leap forward, beyond memories, so to speak. Could it be that just as memories come to life again when we recall them, the results of our actions have a tendency to come back to us? We all know that memories are just waiting to reappear. But could it be the same with the results of past actions? Perhaps experiences in the outer world come toward us because we need to meet them. Regarding such experiences, Steiner asks, "Are they waiting to approach the soul from the outside, just as a memory waits for a reason to approach from the inside?"

This is worth examining. Let us say, for example, that one goes to a certain university. There one meets one's sweetheart, the person with whom one ends up spending many happy years together. On a superficial level, we can say that this meeting was the result of another action, namely the move to the particular university or college. But if such a meeting has happened in your life, a little self-awareness will show that the reality of the experience is far greater than geography or mere chance. When one meets a life partner, there is an overwhelming sense that this is of far greater importance than we can realize in the moment. A voice inside says: What have I done to deserve this? What has destiny brought me?

If my spirit is truly eternal, then the joys and sorrows, the things that happen to me in this life, and the people I meet may depend on actions and interactions that precede this life. Rudolf Steiner stated this concept in his book *Theosophy*: "In this way, we can become able to recognize an experience of destiny as a past action of the soul finding its way to the 'I'.... What we experience as destiny in one lifetime is related to our actions in previous earthly lives."

Thus, every action has consequences. Throwing a stone into a pond near our house delights our son Ionas with a kerplunk, a splash, and ripples. This is a clear example of how phenomena proceed from our every action. Some create ripples that go beyond the confines of one sojourn on Earth. In the case of past actions from other lifetimes, the consequences often come to meet us from without in the form of the people, events, and experiences we encounter.

Why is this so? It has to do with an action's very nature—its anatomy, so to speak. When something is performed as an action, the need to carry out its consequence is impressed on the soul. For instance, if I were to hurt someone, my soul immediately begins to work with the possible consequences. Even when not fully aware of it, we recoil inwardly at what we have done. Some of this soul processing may be unconscious, but it is nevertheless real. It is of course best if one can right away make amends for hurting someone, but this is not always possible. There are situations in which a hurt lingers on, and consequently a yearning grows in the soul to redress the situation. It is inherent in human nature to reclaim equilibrium, to make peace with a situation. Because life is messy and much happens over the years, some things have to wait for another incarnation.

My soul in one lifetime "educates" my spirit to find opportunities for rebalancing in the next life. I then seek out the people and situations that will give me a chance to make amends. This is not just true in the case of negative experiences but also holds true for positive experiences from the past. Good deeds also have consequences. For example, I have often wondered whether the partner we find in this life who brings us joy may have something to do with the quality of interaction we had in a past life.

Thus, in the complex web of destiny, we find ourselves in fascinating situations, go through all sorts of experiences and "chance" encounters, all by way of placing before us the opportunities our souls have desired. Through our past actions the human spirit prepares its own destiny. In a great web of connection, we are linked to each other through multiple lifetimes. Along the way, the spirit grows. What the soul has preserved as memories of life experiences the spirit transforms. Through this, new capacities are developed. Over time we are better able to meet situations with clarity, poise, and compassionate understanding. We are in a better place to help others when we have done our own transformative work.

All this has many implications for our work together in organizations. Do we just bring our baggage to the workplace and dump it on others, or are we personally working with our past experiences so they can be transformed into new capacities for service? Those who have been through the most, have suffered more than others, or have lived life fully in both joy and sorrow often have the most to contribute when a challenge arises at work. Character is formed on the anvil of life.

What we do at work also shapes our character. If one spends years as a nurse or a teacher, a mechanic or an electrician, the nature of the work influences how we fit in to the world around us. We not only see other people through the eyes of a teacher or nurse, but we also become more and more of that role. I can usually spot retired public school teachers before they introduce themselves as such, due to their manner of interacting with my children. Some people are fortunate to have a career, a calling in life, while others are not. This leads us to look more carefully at vocation and the organizational implications of how people find themselves through work.

Appendix 3: Vocation

Why look at vocation in relation to organizational dynamics? There are several reasons that come to mind. First, many people I meet these days are trapped in their jobs. One person said to me just recently: "My company is paying me too well for me to quit." I took the meaning to be that the family is dependent on the income and that doing something else, something more meaningful, would not be possible. Others may not be making quite enough income but are trapped in the benefit plan and are not willing to risk losing the health insurance coverage. No matter what form this takes, the result is that one is unable to listen to the inner stirring, the call for a new arena of work, and life continues in the same, predictable fashion.

Another reason to study vocation is that many people feel caught in the classic struggle between freedom and necessity. The call of freedom may mean starting a new career, moving to a new location, opening a business, or becoming a teacher. The outer form is not as important as the way in which the inner voice prompts us to begin anew. Necessity is that elemental force that binds us to the harsh realities of life, binds us as products of heredity, race, and geographical location among other things. This can take various outer forms, including the notion that the family business requires my continued participation. If I leave, the costs are too high. I am bound by good reasons and bad; my love of family and the necessity of continuing with work now become bittersweet. Those caught in the clutches of necessity often have a love/hate relationship to their work; for if it were all bad, one would be more likely to switch.

Likewise, there are those who wander through life, never really finding their true calling. I spoke with someone in her fifties recently who described this situation. Children have been raised; jobs have been worked; yet there has always been the question: "What am I supposed to do when I grow up?"

Then there are those who have forged ahead, found new careers, even invented new occupations. These folks tend to have one thing in common—they listened to an inner stirring, they took the plunge, and they are so excited about what they are doing that everything else falls into place. Sacrifices are made, loved ones usually stay connected and may even be intimately involved, and a new career unfolds. For some people this may mean opening a restaurant; for others it may mean working with children or inventing new technology. There is a sense of adventure and joy. Where did this new direction come from? How can others gain access to this elixir?

Finally, there are those who want to live several lifetimes at once. Personally, I would do many more things if only there were more hours in the day. Parenting and partnering are often full-time, immensely rewarding occupations. Then there is my love of teaching, the joy of connecting with the wonderful people attracted to Antioch University and the Center for Anthroposophy here in New Hampshire. The field work with schools, collaborative leadership training and consulting, give me raw material out of which I learn to understand the dynamics of groups and organizations. Then there is my thirst for research and writing. If only one had more time for all of the above.

Every moment of the day we are compelled to make choices. Will the outer demands always hold sway? Are there times when we listen to the inner voice as well? With each of the various aspects of life, there is both a reactive and a proactive way of working. Learning to know one's vocation and heeding the call of life can be a tremendous help in achieving success.

When I lead workshops on vocation, I often begin by asking participants to list the physical characteristics that they have inherited from their parents. These may include everything from hair color to height, from facial expressions to health. Once a few people share their lists, I then talk about our connection to heredity. We are given certain physical characteristics thanks to our parents. One's race, birthplace, nationality, culture, physical health, and predisposition to certain illnesses all arise from heredity. This is a fact.

The next question is subtler. What can be "read" in the demeanor and physical expression that is you and not someone else? Are there certain facial expressions, gestures, and habits that you have acquired? Each person has a slightly different way of walking if one takes the time to observe. If we look carefully, we can see the whole personality simply in the way someone walks. Posture is also significant. Here we are not just talking about physical aspects, but the life (etheric) forces that have shaped us. This can be seen in some of the smallest details.

For example, most babies like to "pull in" with a bottle, pacifier, or thumb sucking. As the biological father of three sons I have observed vastly different behaviors just in this small detail. One liked to suck the two middle fingers of his left hand while twiddling his hair with the other hand. Another was a classic thumb sucker, while Ionas, our youngest, caressed his stomach while drinking his bottle. Each gesture was so individual. Even at age four Ionas would complain if I cut his nails too short because then he could not "touch my stomach." The important thing about such observations is to let the phenomena sink in without looking for an immediate interpretation. In regard to these three fellows, what do these gestures tell me? For each distinctive gesture is a window into the soul and the emerging personality.

The third step in the workshop process is to look at the list of physical characteristics and the typical gestures and ask, what has been transformed? Each of us works with life, and over time things change. What has been given from parents or early mannerisms that change as the years go by? It is helpful to see what has been transformed. Let's say a child grows up in a large household with many loud voices competing for attention at mealtimes. The parents argue, even shout at times, yet they clearly love one another deeply. Years later, the child in question has become a quiet, mild-mannered person known for respectful listening. Clearly these changes were self-initiated. This is an example of the third step in the vocational exercise.

Finally, I ask the group to look at biography. What have I done with my life thus far? Can I identify major turning points? This constitutes the last preparatory step before taking on the issue of vocation directly. In the four steps covered in the previous exercises, attention has been given to four aspects of the human being as described in chapter 1 of my book *Organizational Integrity:*

1. Physical: heredity, earthly, the given life situation.
2. Etheric: life forces, that which has formed us, given us characteristic gestures, habits, inner disposition.
3. Astral: overcoming emotional and personal challenges, conscious attempts at transformation, change, making my life my own.
4. "I": my unfolding story, my individuality, my unique self.

These four aspects are interrelated. For example, the physical aspect creates life situations and the "I" transforms these life situations into life's story. Along the way we enter into relationships with people and these connections influence our work, our vocation. Likewise, the etheric forms our inner peculiarities that then show themselves in demeanor, gesture, and posture. This is especially true in the "formative" years of seven to fourteen, when the etheric works most strongly. An example is the rich imaginative life many children have at this age; they can easily accept their characters in a dramatic production with minimal use of costume or makeup. This direct ability to grasp the pictorial and imaginable immediately is the etheric life force at work.

But in the seven-year period that follows, which is the development of the physical into the emotional, the astral body is released and a great struggle ensues. Will I continue in just the way my parents want me to be or can I become something that is just me? The movie *Failure to Launch* treats an exaggerated form of this issue when two aging parents hire a young woman to lure their son, age thirty-five, into finally moving out of their house. Usually, this separation from heredity happens in the teenage years, but our society has in many ways prolonged adolescence. During these transition years the past and future struggle within the young person, with occasional outbursts of rejection and reconnection.

Thus, etheric life forces and the astral of the above four aspects are related, as are the physical and the "I." But there is more to this story. If you place this view of the human being in a time line that stretches far back, even prior to birth, you can begin to appreciate a remarkable statement by Rudolf Steiner when speaking of the characteristic gestures, posture, and demeanor of the child, "A great part of what thus appears in developing children is derived from karma and is the effect of the vocation of their preceding incarnations." If I understand this correctly, the particular characteristics of a child in this life are a result of a past vocation. What occupied numerous working hours of a person in one life has been carried forward into formative elements in the present life. Let us say that a man was a blacksmith in the Middle Ages, spending endless hours working with metal, fire, and physical exertion. This impressed itself on the soul of the person to the degree that, when reincarnated, the gestures of the new life bear an imprint, as it were, of that vocation of the past life. The past work lived on in the etheric and is now imprinted in the person's physical attributes. We are shaped by our work in many unimagined ways.

Then, in the teenage battle to assert "who I am," the vocational karma of the past—such as in my example of the blacksmith—is countered by an equally pressing demand to transform what has been given into something new. One could say that puberty is our only legitimate "crisis." Depending on how this struggle is resolved, the young person will find a new vocation for this life, remain mired in the ambivalence of indecision, or accept a handed down career or job.

Many of our high schools and colleges do not take into account this epic struggle for vocation in the years fourteen to twenty-one. Often, students are expected to declare a major and take courses that specialize in theoretical content areas that have little validity in terms of the search for vocation. Many professors are trained in their subject areas but have minimal understanding of adolescent development.

Waldorf high schools come closer than any place I know in working with the emerging emotional life as well as the ripening intellect. It is when they truly engage the will, be it in a naturalist program, taking apart a car in physics, or building a canoe in preparation for a field trip, that the adolescent really takes hold of life. I remember when my son Thomas came home one night after a class on permutations and combinations with Connie

Gerwin, the math teacher and his advisor at High Mowing School during that time. They had sampled a sumptuous meal together—ten students working on all the possible permutations and combinations of the multicourse feast. He has never forgotten that learning experience. When students are provided with such rich opportunities in high school, they are more likely to connect with the world and future career possibilities.

There are students whose vocational interest happens to fall into a prescribed area, and consequently they may become, for example, enthusiastic engineering students or premed majors. Such students can thrive in college and public universities. Other than in the Waldorf high schools with which I am familiar, our higher educational institutions do not do so well with those struggling to find themselves, especially for those who want to explore "out of the box." Some students experiment with different jobs and lifestyles during their twenties, and perhaps in the face of pressure they even submit to study in an academic institution. Those with healthy instincts often take time off between high school and college, or do a year abroad during the university years.

From a vocational perspective, I advocate for a "thirteenth year" of development transition between twelfth grade high school and college. Recognizing the need to experience different ways of living and learning, students can spend time learning by doing, working with different professionals in the field, trying things out and learning from life. If they undertake academic work, it should be based upon natural interest and a wish to make sense of experiences. The focus could be service learning. Some will find a thirteenth year challenging, but adversity also educates. With improved training for college advisors, we can better help our eighteen-year-olds. Freshmen, especially the boys

I have known at college, are usually at a loss as to know what to do with their sudden freedom. So often our youth have high ideals that are then shattered when they come up against the realities of the world. Coming up against oneself in the workplace, even encountering a certain amount of adversity, schools the soul and ignites the spirit flame of our own unique individuality. In this schooling of life, vocation is uncovered, drawn forth from the clutches of karma. Our subsequent career choices would then more likely be in response to a true calling.

Getting a right vocation is not only important for future career success and family happiness, but has implications for personal health and well-being. Many illnesses today are bred in the hot house of stress. Even though stress is part of everyone's life today, for some, the discrepancy between inner calling and "must-do" work is too great. If you have to go day after day to a job that is totally unfulfilling, something starts to die inside. Apathy and stagnation allow predator forces into the castle of self. In contrast, enthusiasm creates vitality and the strength to do the impossible. One modality slays forces in the soul, the other recreates. Doctors and others who work with illness can attest to the effect of stress and dejection on physical health. Lack of vocation is frequently manifest in heart disease. The heart, as will be described in greater detail later, is the "sun" center, the place where our most sacred wishes are housed and nourished. When we cannot circulate in good ways with our vocational work life, our physical circulation can suffer. Our interactions with others and the world in general can either help or hinder our physical health. Living one's passion, heeding the call of vocation, is good for body, soul, and spirit. Rudolf Steiner spoke to this connection of vocation and physical health when he said, "If we go more deeply into this, the fact becomes apparent that a person's external career in one incarnation, when it is not merely a career but also an inner vocation, passes over in the next incarnation into the inward shaping of their bodily organs."

Thus, vocation has importance beyond a career path. It can literally shape our organs. If we can achieve a complete picture of the human being in a state of health, we will find clues for developing and then sustaining organizational wellbeing.*

---

* For more on this topic, see Finser, *Organizational Integrity: How to Apply the Wisdom of the Body to Develop Healthy Organizations*, from which appendix 3 was taken.

SELECT BIBLIOGRAPHY

Cohen, Warren Lee. *Raising the Soul: Practical Exercises for Personal Development*. London: Rudolf Steiner Press, 2006.

Finser, Torin M. *In Search of Ethical Leadership: If not now, when?* Great Barrington, MA: SteinerBooks, 2003.

———. *Initiative: A Rosicrucian Path of Leadership*. Great Barrington, MA: SteinerBooks, 2011.

———. *Organizational Integrity: How to Apply the Wisdom of the Body to Develop Healthy Organizations*. Great Barrington, MA: SteinerBooks, 2007.

———. *School as a Journey: The Eight-Year Odyssey of a Waldorf Teacher and His Class*. Hudson, NY: Anthroposophic Press, 1995.

———. *School Renewal: A Spiritual Journey for Change*. Great Barrington, MA: SteinerBooks, 1999.

———. *A Second Classroom: Parent-Teacher Relationships in a Waldorf School*. Great Barrington, MA: SteinerBooks, 2014.

———. *Silence Is Complicity: A Call to Let Teachers Improve Our Schools through Action Research—Not NCLB*. Great Barrington, MA: SteinerBooks, 2007.

Hughes, Gertrude Reif. *More Radiant than the Sun: A Handbook for Working with Steiner's Meditations and Exercises*. Great Barrington, MA: SteinerBooks, 2013.

Klocek, Dennis. *The Seer's Handbook: A Guide to Higher Perception*. Great Barrington, MA: SteinerBooks, 2004.

Kühlewind, Georg. *From Normal to Healthy: Paths to the Liberation of Consciousness*. Hudson, NY: Lindisfarne Books, 1998.

———. *The Gentle Will: Guidelines for Creative Consciousness*. Great Barrington, MA: Lindisfarne Books, 2011.

———. *The Light of the "I": Guidelines for Meditation*. Great Barrington, MA: SteinerBooks, 2008.

———. *Working with Anthroposophy: The Practice of Thinking*. Hudson, NY: Anthroposophic Press, 1992.

Lindenberg, Christoph. *Rudolf Steiner: A Biography*. Great Barrington, MA: SteinerBooks, 2012.

Lipson, Michael. *Group Meditation*. Great Barrington, MA: SteinerBooks, 2011.

———. *Stairway of Surprise: Six Steps to a Creative Life.* Great
Barrington, MA: SteinerBooks, 2002.

Lowndes, Florin. *Enlivening the Chakra of the Heart: The
Fundamental Spiritual Exercises of Rudolf Steiner.* London:
Rudolf Steiner Press, 2000.

McDermott, Robert. *The New Essential Steiner: An Introduction
to Rudolf Steiner for the 21st Century.* Great Barrington, MA:
Lindisfarne Books, 2009.

Romero, Lisa. *Developing the Self: Through the Inner Work Path in the
Light of Anthroposophy.* Great Barrington, MA: SteinerBooks,
2015.

———. *The Inner Work Path: A Foundation for Meditative Practice in
the Light of Anthroposophy.* Great Barrington, MA: SteinerBooks,
2014.

Selg, Peter. *Rudolf Steiner, Life and Work: 1961–1925* (8 vols.). Great
Barrington, MA: SteinerBooks, 2012–.

Steiner, Rudolf. *Anthroposophical Leading Thoughts: Anthroposophy as
a Path of Knowledge: The Michael Mystery.* London: Rudolf Steiner
Press, 1973.

———. *Anthroposophy in Everyday Life: Practical Training in Thought,
Overcoming Nervousness, Facing Karma, The Four Temperaments.*
Hudson, NY: Anthroposophic Press, 1995.

———. *Autobiography: Chapters in the Course of My Life, 1861–1907.*
Great Barrington, MA: SteinerBooks, 2000.

———. *Christianity as Mystical Fact: And the Mysteries of Antiquity.*
Great Barrington, MA: SteinerBooks, 1997.

———. *The Calendar of the Soul.* Hudson, NY: Anthroposophic Press,
1988.

———. *Esoteric Development: Lectures and Writings.* Great Barrington,
MA: SteinerBooks, 2003.

———. *First Steps in Inner Development.* Hudson, NY: Anthroposophic
Press, 1999.

———. *Founding a Science of the Spirit.* London: Rudolf Steiner Press,
1999.

———. *Goethe's Theory of Knowledge: An Outline of the Epistemology
of His Worldview.* Great Barrington, MA: SteinerBooks, 2008.

———. *Guidance in Esoteric Training: From the Esoteric School.* London:
Rudolf Steiner Press, 1998.

———. *How to Know Higher Worlds: A Modern Path of Initiation.*
Hudson, NY: Anthroposophic Press, 1994.

——. *Intuitive Thinking as a Spiritual Path: A Philosophy of Freedom.* Hudson, NY: Anthroposophic Press, 1995.

——. *An Outline of Esoteric Science.* Hudson, NY: Anthroposophic Press, 1997.

——. *A Psychology of Body, Soul, and Spirit: Anthroposophy, Psychosophy, Pneumatosophy.* Hudson, NY: Anthroposophic Press, 1999.

——. *Six Steps in Self-Development: The "Supplementary Exercises."* London: Rudolf Steiner Press, 2011.

——. *Soul Exercises: Word and Symbol Meditations.* Great Barrington, MA: SteinerBooks, 2014.

——. *The Spiritual Guidance of the Individual and Humanity: Some Results of Spiritual-Scientific Research into Human History and Development.* Hudson, NY: Anthroposophic Press, 1992.

——. *The Spiritual Hierarchies and the Physical World: Zodiac, Planets, and Cosmos.* Great Barrington, MA: SteinerBooks, 2008.

——. *The Stages of Higher Knowledge: Imagination, Inspiration, Intuition.* Great Barrington, MA: SteinerBooks, 2009.

——. *Start Now! A Book of Soul and Spiritual Exercises.* Great Barrington, MA: SteinerBooks, 2002.

——. *Strengthening the Will: The "Review Exercises."* London: Rudolf Steiner Press, 2011.

——. *Theosophy: An Introduction to the Spiritual Processes in Human Life and in the Cosmos.* Hudson, NY: Anthroposophic Press, 1994.

——. *Verses and Meditations.* London: Rudolf Steiner Press, 2004.

——. *A Way of Self-Knowledge: And the Threshold of the Spiritual World.* Hudson, NY: Anthroposophic Press, 1999.

Unger, Carl. *The Language of the Consciousness Soul: A Guide to Rudolf Steiner's "Leading Thoughts."* Great Barrington, MA: SteinerBooks, 2012.

——. *Steiner's Theosophy and Principles of Spiritual Science.* Great Barrington, MA: SteinerBooks, 2014.

Zajonc, Arthur. *Meditation as Contemplative Inquiry: When Knowing Becomes Love.* Great Barrington, MA: Lindisfarne Books, 2008.

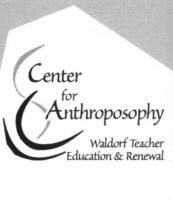

Waldorf High School Teacher Education Program

Douglas Gerwin, Program Chair
A graduate-level summers program leading to a Waldorf high school teaching certificate in:
Arts/Art History — English — History — Life Sciences
Mathematics — Pedagogical Eurythmy — Physical Sciences

Foundation Studies in Anthroposophy and the Arts

Barbara Richardson, Coordinator
Basic anthroposophical principles and artistic exercises that lay the groundwork
for becoming a Waldorf teacher. Individually mentored studies available.

Renewal Courses

Karine Munk Finser, Coordinator
Two weeks of five-day retreats for Waldorf teachers and other professionals
seeking personal rejuvenation and social renewal through anthroposophical study,
artistic immersion, good food, and fun.

For a complete listing of courses please visit *www.centerforanthroposophy.org*
Summer Programs Located in beautiful Wilton, New Hampshire
603-654-2566 • info@centerforanthroposophy.org

Moving through our days and pondering what we meet, it is easy to see that all is not well with the world. Our foundational structures — economic, health, environmental, social — reflect a loss of humane values. Many wonder if humanity has the courage and imagination to evolve new forms.

Inspired by Rudolf Steiner's work and vision a century ago, anthroposophists seek to engage the better nature and higher potentials in themselves and all human beings. In terms Steiner used as a young man, this involves our becoming not just knowers ("critics") or doers ("activists"), but **the one who matters most of all: the knowing doer"** — the thoughtful helper, the caring researcher, the conscious human being.

Rudolf Steiner developed his own remarkable abilities into **anthroposophy**, a heightened and disciplined **"consciousness of our humanity"** which forms a body of resources and initiatives to support healthy individual growth and resilient, creative, and caring communities. In the USA, the non-profit, non-sectarian **Anthroposophical Society in America** works to further this vision. Through more intimate personal reflection and study, group collaboration in research and community building, and devoted service to others, members try to *become the change* humanity needs, each according to her or his conscience and inspiration.

"People must come closer to one another than they used to do," Steiner observed, "each becoming an awakener of everyone he or she meets." **E-mail** (information@anthroposophy.org) or **call** (888.757.2742) for a free copy of *being human*, our quarterly magazine, information on programs and webinars, and how to join in and support this work. And go to **www.anthroposophy.org** where you can find out more about the many faces and facets of anthroposophy today.

connecting
serving
deepening

anthroposophy.org

Dear Readers,

Waldorf Education celebrates over 95 years of growth worldwide with its centenary birthday coming up in 2019. For a third of that time, the Waldorf Teacher Education Program at Antioch University New England has been meeting the growing and tremendous need for trained Waldorf teachers.

Over the years, hundreds of our graduates have spread out all over North America and beyond. While loyally devoted to their individual schools, they also form an Antioch network of alumni who stay in touch with one another, host interns and at times return to our summer campus in Wilton, New Hampshire, for refreshment in renewal courses. At Antioch, relationships are formed that can last a lifetime.

The Waldorf Teacher Education Program is uniquely integrated into a fully accredited university known for its values of social change and justice and for cutting-edge methods in professional transformation. The program offers a year-round option (including two summers) in Keene, New Hampshire, for pre-service teachers including elementary public school teacher certification; a three summer sequence option for in-service and pre-service teachers living at a distance; and a two summer Healing Education option for experienced Waldorf teachers and advanced anthroposophic practitioners.

All options unfold through a combination of group coursework, independent study, and practical experience. Main features include:
- In-depth study of how the Waldorf education meets the child's cognitive, emotional, moral and therapeutic needs
- In-depth exploration of the theoretical foundations of Waldorf education and anthroposophy
- Artistic courses which develop creative capacities for application in the art of teaching, counseling and administration as well as for personal development
- 15 course instructors with fresh insights from direct practice in schools and related centers
- Internship and practicum experiences that consolidate a student's learning
- Small class learning communities to which the student contributes personal experience, insight, and research
- Professional seminars to reflect on direct experiences and practice
- Exhilarating and demanding summer intensive sessions in a retreat setting on the scenic hilltop campuses of two adjacent Waldorf schools in Wilton, New Hampshire
- Personal, social, and professional connections with individuals and schools that last a lifetime

Each summer, Antioch's Waldorf faculty members welcome more than 100 students from all over the continent—most recently from China, Haiti, and Iran—to study with us in New Hampshire.

Please visit us and attend a class! For more information, contact Laura Andrews at admissions. ane@antioch.edu, (800) 552-8380, or visit antiochne.edu/waldorf.

Arthur Auer, MEd
Director

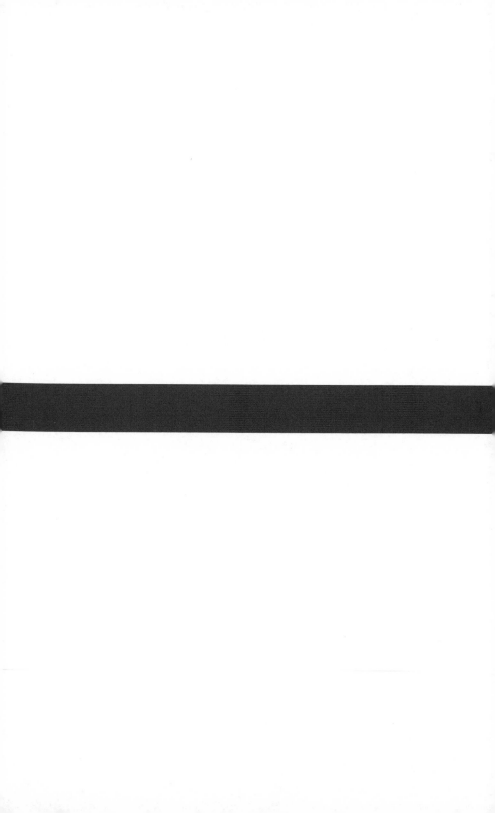